The Heel
of the Conqueror

By the Editors of Time-Life Books

Alexandria, Virginia

TIME
LIFE®

Time-Life Books is a division of
Time Life Inc., a wholly owned subsidiary of
The Time Inc. Book Company
Time-Life Books

Managing Editor: Thomas H. Flaherty
Director of Editorial Resources:
Elise D. Ritter-Clough
Director of Photography and Research:
John Conrad Weiser
Editorial Board: Dale M. Brown, Roberta Conlan,
Laura Foreman, Lee Hassig, Jim Hicks, Blaine
Marshall, Rita Thievon Mullin, Henry Woodhead

PUBLISHER: Joseph J. Ward

Associate Publisher: Ann M. Mirabito
Editorial Director: Russell B. Adams, Jr.
Marketing Director: Anne C. Everhart
Director of Design: Louis Klein
Production Manager: Prudence G. Harris
Supervisor of Quality Control: James King

Editorial Operations
Production: Celia Beattie
Library: Louise D. Forstall
Computer Composition: Deborah G. Tait
(Manager), Monika D. Thayer,
Janet Barnes Syring, Lillian Daniels

The Cover: A German soldier wearing an Iron Cross
confronts an elderly woman in the town of Romilly
in northern France in June 1940, when Wehrmacht
forces were sweeping through western Europe.
During nearly five years of war, the citizens of the
occupied countries struggled to maintain a normal
life in the face of increasingly harsh oppression by
the German overlords.

This volume is one of a series that chronicles
the rise and eventual fall of Nazi Germany. Other
books in the series include:
The SS
Fists of Steel
Storming to Power
The New Order
The Reach for Empire
Lightning War
Wolf Packs
Conquest of the Balkans
Afrikakorps
The Center of the Web
Barbarossa
War on the High Seas
The Twisted Dream
The Road to Stalingrad
The Shadow War

The Third Reich

SERIES EDITOR: Henry Woodhead
Series Administrator: Philip Brandt George
Editorial Staff for *The Heel of the Conqueror:*
Senior Art Director: Raymond Ripper
Picture Editor: Jane Jordan
Text Editor: John Newton
Writers: Stephanie A. Lewis, Barbara C. Mallen
Associate Editors/Research: Oobie Gleysteen,
Karen Monks, Trudy Pearson
Assistant Editor/Research: Katherine Griffin
Assistant Art Director: Lorraine D. Rivard
Senior Copy Coordinator: Anne Farr
Picture Coordinator: Jennifer Iker
Editorial Assistant: Alan Schager

Special Contributors: Ronald H. Bailey,
John Clausen, Kenneth C. Danforth, George G.
Daniels, Betsy Frankel, Lydia Preston Hicks,
Richard W. Murphy, Peter Pocock, David S.
Thomson (text); Martha Lee Beckington, Anthony
J. Sheehan, Marilyn Murphy Terrell (research);
Roy Nanovic (index)

Correspondents: Elisabeth Kraemer-Singh
(Bonn), Christine Hinze (London), Christina
Lieberman (New York), Maria Vincenza Aloisi
(Paris), Ann Natanson (Rome). Valuable
assistance was also provided by: Barbara Gevene
Hertz (Copenhagen), Judy Aspinall (London),
Wibo Vandelinde (Netherlands), Katheryn White
(New York), Dag Christensen (Oslo).

First printing. Printed in U.S.A.

Published simultaneously in Canada.
School and library distribution by Silver Burdett
Company, Morristown, New Jersey 07960.

TIME-LIFE is a trademark of Time Warner Inc.
U.S.A.

Library of Congress Cataloging in
Publication Data
The Heel of the conqueror / by the editors of
Time-Life Books.
    p.   cm. — (The Third Reich)
    Includes bibliographical references and index.
    ISBN 0-8094-7012-8 (trade)
    ISBN 0-8094-7013-6 (lib. bdg.)
    1. World War, 1939-1945—Occupied territories.
2. World War, 1939-1945—Underground
movements—Europe. 3. World War, 1939-
1945—Collaborationists—Europe. 4. Europe—
History—1918-1945
I. Time-Life Books. II. Series.
D802.E9H38 1991   940.53'36—dc20   90-19703

Other Publications:

For information on and a full description of any
of the Time-Life Books series listed above, please
call 1-800-621-7026 or write:
Reader Information
Time-Life Customer Service
P.O. Box C-32068
Richmond, Virginia 23261-2068

General Consultants

Col. John R. Elting, USA (Ret.), former associate professor at West Point, has written
or edited some twenty books, including
*Swords around a Throne, The Superstrate-
gists,* and *American Army Life,* as well as
Battles for Scandinavia in the Time-Life
Books World War II series. He was chief con-
sultant to the Time-Life series The Civil War.

Norman Rich, PhD, Professor Emeritus of
History at Brown University, specializes in
German political and diplomatic history. A
Guggenheim and Fulbright fellow, he has
also taught at Bryn Mawr College and Mich-
igan State University. He is the author of numerous scholarly articles and several books,
including his two-volume *Hitler's War Aims*
and *Friedrich von Holstein: Politics and Di-
plomacy in the Era of Bismarck and Wilhelm
II,* also in two volumes.

Contents

A Shadow across Europe

While the Wehrmacht overran western Europe during the spring of 1940, no one back home in Germany watched with keener interest than those who stood to profit most from the new conquests. The tycoons of the aggressor nation waited impatiently to claim the booty of the defeated countries once the shooting stopped. A Bavarian art dealer named Artur Rümann later recalled a lunch with several prominent industrialists in an exclusive eating club in Düsseldorf, the business center of the great coal- and steel-producing Ruhr valley. It was 2:00 p.m. on Saturday, May 18, and the businessmen interrupted their meal to listen to a radio broadcast of the latest war bulletins.

German forces had overwhelmed the small and unprepared Netherlands. At that very moment, the diners learned, panzers from General Gerd von Rundstedt's Army Group A were two-thirds of the way across northern France, racing for the English Channel, and General Fedor von Bock's Army Group B had reached the Dender River, halfway across Belgium.

One of the men at the table produced a map of the Netherlands, and as the radio announcer called out the placenames, eyes darted back and forth to pinpoint the Dutch holdings now in German hands. "There is Müller," said one, pointing to a spot on the map. "He is yours." Said another, "There is Schmidt. He has two plants; we will have him arrested." One of the diners, young Alfred Krupp, scion of the famous munitions family, said to another, "This factory is yours." While the others continued their vigil over the map, one of the moguls telephoned his office. He wanted to apply for special passports so that he and his colleagues might go and see for themselves.

Holland had scarcely surrendered, and already these industrialists were dividing up the spoils. And they were not alone. Throughout the Reich, a host of expectant Germans—military and public officials as well as private entrepreneurs—were poised to pounce on the newly occupied lands.

Four months earlier, during the so-called *Sitzkrieg*, or phony war, that followed the conquest of Poland, Hermann Göring, in his role as head of

Flanked by Reichsführer-SS Heinrich Himmler *(right)* and Reichskommissar of the Netherlands Dr. Artur Seyss-Inquart, Dutch "Shadow Führer" Anton Mussert observes activities at a pro-German rally in Holland in 1942. To Mussert, a puppet administrator in Holland's occupation government, Hitler was "the liberator of Europe."

Hitler's motorcade crosses the Rhine into Alsace following the Wehrmacht's conquest of France in June 1940. Flush with victory, the Führer conducted inspection tours of the decimated fortifications along the Maginot Line, stopping frequently to congratulate his triumphant troops.

the Reich's Four-Year Plan, had spelled out Hitler's economic policy for western Europe. "The Führer is firmly convinced that he will succeed in reaching a decision on the war in 1940 by making a big attack in the west," Göring informed General Georg Thomas, chief of the military economy and armaments department of the armed forces high command. Then Göring referred to the resources of the countries that Hitler expected to capture: "The decision follows to exploit everything to the utmost in 1940, and to exploit the raw-material reserves at their expense in later years."

Thomas made the necessary preparations, organizing military economic staffs and field units, called *Wirtschaftstruppen,* to accompany the invading forces to locate, catalog, and seize essential goods. Their orders called for them to ship "trainload after trainload" back to German factories or to confiscated finishing plants within the occupied zones.

The *Wirtschaftstruppen* would have no trouble filling the freight cars. In two lightning campaigns lasting less than eleven weeks, from the collapse of Denmark on April 9 to the fall of France on June 22, Hitler's armies overran no fewer than six countries. These nations—Luxembourg, the Netherlands, Belgium, Norway, Denmark, and France—had lucrative agricultural and industrial resources and an aggregate population of nearly 66 million. Their people ranked among the best educated, highest skilled, and most productive in the world.

In the next five years, the Germans would bleed the captive countries of their wealth and resources and hold their people in thrall. Many in the occupied lands would resist the German yoke, others would collaborate, but the majority would simply try to get on with their lives and endure as best they could. It would not be easy. Thousands of Europeans were uprooted and sent to Germany to perform forced labor; thousands more were shipped to the Nazi death camps. At home, as the war worsened, the German presence grew more oppressive and the personal deprivations multiplied. By the end, as the Allied invasion made much of western Europe a battleground, many people had reached the point of starvation, many more were homeless, and all faced a perilous future amid the wreckage created by Hitler's ambitions.

Hitler, at the outset, was ill-prepared to administer his conquests. For all the Nazi rhetoric about shaping a new order, the Führer had given little thought to what form it might take in western Europe. Most of his pronouncements had focused on "purifying" the Reich by removing the Jews from German soil and on seizing vast new *Lebensraum,* or living space, from the "racially inferior" Slavs in the east. He had not determined which areas were to be cleared and colonized and which peoples were to be absorbed

through a process of Germanization. In 1940, his propaganda minister, Joseph Goebbels, admitted, "If anyone asks today how we imagine the new Europe, we must say we do not know."

Unlike his attack on Poland or the eventual invasion of Russia, Hitler's drive westward was motivated by strategic, rather than ideological, concerns. He decided to attack Norway to protect his lifeline of iron ore flowing from neutral Sweden and to prevent the British navy from bottling up his high-seas fleet in the Baltic. Denmark was the steppingstone to Norway. He attacked Germany's perennial foe, France, to safeguard the vital Ruhr district and protect his rear during the ultimate *Drang nach Osten*, the impending drive east that would guarantee the security of the German *Volk* for all time. Luxembourg and Belgium lay astride the invasion routes into France. He seized Holland as part of the attack on France and to establish air and submarine bases for an assault against England—should the British refuse to settle the war by diplomatic means. As for the rest of western Europe, Franco's Spain was assumed to be friendly; Portugal and Switzerland offered no strategic benefits and, like Sweden, remained neutral.

Hitler governed his new empire in the west as he had determined military strategy—by improvisation. There was no uniform policy, even though each occupation overlord had the same task: the pacification of the country and the mobilization of its economy to furnish the maximum amount of foodstuffs and matériel for Germany's war economy. While relying as much as possible on the indigenous governments to carry out day-to-day administration, Hitler assigned to each country the type of control—military or civilian, direct or indirect—that appeared least likely to interfere with his prosecution of the war.

A patchwork of overlapping jurisdictions and responsibilities evolved, similar to the jumbled nature of the Reich government itself. As in Germany, much of this was deliberate, designed by Hitler to prevent the army, the SS, or any other agency or administrator from acquiring sufficient power to challenge his authority.

The simplest form of control was incorporation into the Reich. Although Hitler may have had such a fate in mind for much of the conquered territories, he decreed outright annexation for only three small areas in eastern Belgium, containing fewer than 15,000 people. Formerly German, the provinces of Eupen, Malmédy, and Moresnet had been awarded to Belgium after World War I. "The districts separated from the Reich by the Versailles dictate are once again in German possession," Hitler proclaimed, scarcely a week after his panzers swept through them. "At heart, they have always remained united with Germany. They are therefore not even temporarily to be regarded and treated as occupied enemy territory."

The Führer attached the areas to the Prussian province of Aachen and gave citizenship to all inhabitants of German descent. In February of 1941, he granted them seats in the Reichstag "in order to give visible expression to the reunion of the territories with the Greater German Reich."

He placed three larger areas contiguous to Germany under special civilian administration preparatory to incorporation into the Reich. These included Luxembourg, a constitutional grand duchy with an area of not quite 1,000 square miles (slightly smaller than Rhode Island) and a population of about 300,000, and the French provinces of Alsace and Lorraine, which embraced 5,607 square miles and nearly two million people. Luxembourg's historical links with Germany dated back to the Holy Roman Empire of medieval times. Alsace and Lorraine also had old ties. They had been lost to France in the seventeenth century, regained in 1871 after the Franco-Prussian War, and lost again after the Great War.

Hitler appointed a gauleiter from a German district across the Rhine to administer each region. These high-ranking party officials were responsible for all political, economic, and civil defense activities in their districts and reported directly to the Führer.

Despite Luxembourg's Germanic roots, Hitler at first called the tiny nation "enemy territory" and placed it under military control. He was angered by the Luxembourgers' continued resistance and by the flight into exile of Grand Duchess Charlotte and her ministers. But when key civil servants helped restore order, Hitler relented. He brought in Gustav Simon, the gauleiter of Koblenz-Trier, to install a civilian government and begin a Germanization program. In one of his first official statements, Simon told the Luxembourgers that their future was sealed: "On the day when the first grave for a German hero-soldier was dug, we made the following decision: This land was won and will be kept by German blood and therefore will remain German for all eternity." Luxembourg, he said, would be ruled as German land that had been robbed of its essential Germanic character.

Gustav Simon, appointed head of the German civil government in occupied Luxembourg, works at his desk following the Reich's invasion of the grand duchy in May 1940. Answerable directly to Hitler, Simon was charged with recovering "the former German Reichsland Luxembourg for the German Reich."

German replaced French as the official language. "Luxembourg is too proud of its heritage and its native language to be the parrot of France," Simon declared. He oversaw the introduction of Nazi textbooks into the schools, the reorganization of the courts along German lines, and the integration of the post office and other public utilities into the Reich's systems. He banned all political organizations except the Nazi party and made young men of military age subject to Germany's draft. Younger men and boys had to join the paramilitary Reich Labor Service or the Hitler Youth, depending on their age. He forced the Luxembourgers to Germanize their names and change all placenames, street signs, building names, and even tombstone inscriptions into German.

Representatives of Heinrich Himmler's SS soon arrived to assist. For Himmler, Germanization primarily meant ridding Luxembourg of foreigners and people of mixed blood. As a first step, he ordered his chief of the Liaison Office for Ethnic Germans, Werner Lorenz, to compile racial lists of the entire population. By the autumn of 1941, Lorenz had identified 7,000 individuals who, though of proper German stock, lacked sufficient national socialist zeal. Himmler ordered them shipped off to occupied Poland and the protectorate of Bohemia and Moravia, where they posed less of a threat and could receive political orientation. He replaced the deportees with ethnic Germans from the South Tyrol. To help accommodate the new immigrants, he confiscated the property of Luxembourg's 3,000 Jews.

Nazifying Alsace and Lorraine presented a greater challenge because of the region's complicated history. Hitler had always considered Bismarck's legislative efforts to Germanize the districts weak and ineffectual. He admired the way the French had reimposed their culture and customs after 1918 and was determined to go them one better. "If we want to make these into authentic German provinces," he declared, "we must drive out all those who do not voluntarily accept the fact that they are Germans."

The Führer gave the job to two trusted members of the Nazi old guard. Robert Wagner, the gauleiter of Baden who took over Alsace, had marched with Hitler in the Beer Hall Putsch and served time in Landsberg prison; Lorraine's overseer, Joseph Bürckel, the gauleiter of the Saar-Palatinate, was an expert in Nazi annexation policy. He had been the party's plenipotentiary for the 1935 plebiscite that regained the Saar and served as *Reichskommissar* (Reich commissioner) for the 1938 reunion with Austria.

Following Simon's example, the two gauleiters Germanized the governments, legal systems, educational systems, and economies of their districts. Wagner even banned the beret traditionally worn by peasants and workmen in an effort to make the Alsatian men look less Gallic. In addition, Wagner and Bürckel orchestrated a series of mass deportations to get rid

One month after the Germans overran the province of Lorraine in eastern France in June 1940, residents of Metz seem unperturbed by the nearby German soldier and the Nazi flag atop the city's medieval fortress. By mid-August, however, the Reich's belligerent Germanization of the region had aroused the Lorrainers' intense resentment.

of racial and political undesirables. Wagner expelled 105,000 Jews and pro-French citizens into unoccupied France; Bürckel prepared a similar exodus involving another 100,000 people.

The deportations caused a minor uproar in high Nazi circles. Although the Führer approved the action, Himmler did not. Charging Wagner and Bürckel with wastefully giving away redeemable racial stock to Germany's age-old enemy, the SS chieftain drew up new resettlement guidelines based on what he considered to be proper Nazi principles. Henceforward, he said, Wagner and Bürckel should expel only the lesser breeds, meaning Jews, Gypsies, blacks, criminals, the mentally ill, and "all other trash that does not belong to us on the basis of blood." Alsatians and Lorrainers with proper lineage but improper political ideas were to be resettled in Germany or in eastern Europe where they could acquire appreciation for national socialism. Those who persisted in proclaiming loyalty to France were to be sent to concentration camps.

The exigencies of the war in Russia postponed the full enactment of Himmler's fantastic scheme. Nonetheless, the SS uprooted thousands of Alsatians and Lorrainers—despite the drain it caused on Germany's labor pool and the pressure it placed on its badly overloaded railroad network.

By contrast, German control of Denmark could scarcely have been less heavy-handed—at first. The Danish government's swift acceptance of Hit-

ler's surrender ultimatum of April 9, 1940, earned the Danes the most lenient form of Nazi rule anywhere. Under the terms of surrender, Germany guaranteed Danish independence and territorial sovereignty. The king, cabinet, and parliament were allowed to continue their constitutional duties, and relations between the two countries were carried on through normal diplomatic channels.

Although the Danish people disliked the Germans and resented their presence, they could appreciate the advantages they enjoyed. The arrangement also benefited the Germans. Besides keeping the population relatively content and cooperative, it was a useful sop to world opinion. The Danish "model protectorate" countered the impression among neutral nations, especially the United States, that the terrible abuses of power in Poland were the typical consequences of German occupation.

Hitler appointed as his chief representative the ambassador to Denmark, Cecil von Renthe-Fink, a career diplomat who had served in Copenhagen before the Nazis came to power. Renthe-Fink reported to Foreign Minister Joachim von Ribbentrop. With a civilian staff of only 200 Germans, he oversaw all nonmilitary matters. The Danish armed forces and police remained on duty, necessitating only a token occupation force.

Renthe-Fink often found himself in the peculiar position of negotiating with the elected representatives of a minor nation on soil occupied by the mighty army of the Third Reich. There were, however, limits to German forbearance. At the "suggestion" of German officials, the Danish government imposed censorship on press and radio. And when the cabinet hesitated to sign the Anti-Comintern Pact—a paper instrument against communism—Renthe-Fink exacted quick compliance by threatening to treat Denmark like an occupied nation.

Hitler chafed under the arrangement. He distrusted diplomats like Renthe-Fink and detested the notion of having to negotiate with a parliamentary democracy. He wanted to depose King Christian X and replace him with the leader of the country's tiny National Socialist party, Fritz Clausen. In September 1942, Hitler was further rankled when his telegram of congratulations to King Christian on his seventy-second birthday brought only a terse acknowledgment.

Hitler interpreted this as evidence of Danish arrogance. Despite an apology from the Danish government, he decided to crack down. He replaced General Erich Lüdke, the easygoing German military commander, with a tough Nazi, General Hermann von Hanneken. He also got rid of Renthe-Fink in favor of SS Major General Werner Best. The thirty-nine-year-old Best appeared to be the ideal choice. As chief legal adviser to the Gestapo and deputy to Heinrich Himmler, he had attempted to give le-

Denmark's King Christian X greets a subject during a morning horseback ride through Copenhagen *(top left)*, a habit that the monarch practiced to tacitly affirm Danish sovereignty. At top right, in a show of regal resistance, King Christian ignores the salutes of two German soldiers. Below, flag-waving revelers join in celebrating the King's seventy-second birthday on September 26, 1942. Such patriotic displays irked the Germans, who soon outlawed all demonstrations of nationalism.

gitimacy to the depredations of Himmler's far-flung security apparatus. More recently he had served on the staff of the German military commander in occupied France. Hitler instructed his new plenipotentiary to treat Denmark like a German province.

Instead, Best performed more like his predecessor, Renthe-Fink. He pursued what he called a "policy of understanding" aimed at maintaining the flow of vital Danish agricultural and industrial products to Germany. The light touch was not only working but was in keeping with his own convictions. Before his appointment, Best predicted: "The Danes will adjust to the new order in Europe as the people of Iceland once did to Christianity: not as a result of force or propaganda, but through the cold-blooded realization that this course cannot be avoided."

Following orders, Best persuaded King Christian to dismiss the Socialist prime minister Vilhelm Buhl and approve the formation of a new government under the ostensibly pro-German foreign minister, Erik Scavenius. But in March 1943, as a gesture of conciliation to the Danes and perhaps to prove his point with Berlin, Best permitted nationwide parliamentary elections—the only such free balloting held in German-occupied Europe. The National Socialists of Hitler's would-be chief of state Fritz Clausen won less than three percent of the vote.

The atmosphere changed in Denmark during the summer of 1943 as Mussolini fell to the Allied invasion of Italy and the Danes began to realize that the Axis might not win the war after all. Protest strikes and incidents of sabotage racked the country. Hanneken called for repression. Best counseled restraint and, as a result, was summoned to Berlin for a tongue-lashing by Ribbentrop. He returned to Copenhagen—"a broken man," said an aide—with orders to submit ultimatums that the ministers of the Danish government would surely reject. They did, and on August 29 Hanneken's forces dissolved parliament, placed the king under guard, disarmed the army and the navy, and imposed martial law.

Best sent a plea to Himmler to dispatch SS police to back up his authority. Himmler complied, but, in typical fashion, used the opportunity to strengthen his own power. He sent his former chief of the Central Office for Race and Resettlement, SS Lieut. General Günther Pancke, and exempted him from Best's authority. By November 1943, a clumsy German troika of Best, Pancke, and Hanneken ruled Denmark, and the country began to degenerate into the kind of oppressive police state that proved to be the rule elsewhere in occupied Europe.

In neighboring Norway and in Holland, Hitler from the beginning exercised a far more direct form of control. He appointed a Reichskommissar for each

Werner Best *(far right)*, Denmark's newly appointed Reich plenipotentiary, poses in 1942 with Erik Scavenius, the Danish foreign minister who became the country's premier. By replacing the existing Danish government with the Nazi hard-liner Best and the ardently pro-German Scavenius, Berlin hoped to stem the country's rising insurrectionist tide.

country and gave him extraordinary powers to supervise the existing government or create a new one, and even to legislate by decree. The commissioner was to retain direct authority over every aspect of the occupation except the German military and report directly to the Führer.

Hitler originally had intended to establish for Norway the kind of relatively benign oversight that existed in Denmark for much of the war. But the Norwegians refused to cooperate. For two months during the spring of 1940, they vigorously resisted the German invasion with the aid of expeditionary forces sent by the British and the French. King Haakon VII and his cabinet, instead of remaining in Oslo as Hitler had expected, fled north and then to England, where they instituted a government-in-exile.

Hitler selected Josef Terboven as Reichskommissar for Norway. A former bank employee who had joined the Nazi party in the late 1920s, Terboven rose rapidly to become gauleiter of Essen and administrator of the Rhine Province. He was a pale, bespectacled man with an icy manner and a reputation for brutal energy and ambition.

During that first summer of 1940, Terboven undertook a drastic overhaul of the government, seeking ministers who would be pliable yet capable of controlling the citizenry. By late September, he cajoled the Norwegian parliament, known as the Storting, into deposing the exiled king. Informing Berlin that Norway could now be treated like a "conquered province," he proceeded to dissolve parliament, name a government of pro-German ministers, and abolish all political parties except the Nasjonal Samling, or National Assembly. Founded in 1933, the party was modeled on the Nazis, who had subsidized it before the war. Of the thirteen ministers selected by Terboven, nine belonged to the Nasjonal Samling or supported it.

The party's founder and leader, Vidkun Quisling, however, was not among the appointees. Quisling, who had personally invited Hitler to invade Norway and whose very name would become synonymous with traitor, already had demonstrated his political ineptitude. A one-time career army officer and defense minister, he had proclaimed himself head of the government on April 9, the day of the invasion, only to be shelved by the Germans six days later when he failed to rally popular support. Hitler still hoped to salvage Quisling, and he ordered Terboven to pour in funds and advice to strengthen his party.

When Terboven formed the new pro-German government, Quisling professed indifference toward being a minister, and the Reichskommissar took him at his word. Almost from the beginning, the two men were pitted in a power struggle. Terboven undermined the Norwegian whenever he could by playing off rivals in his own party against him. One, Jonas Lie, a veteran police official and a writer of popular detective stories, was appointed to

the powerful position of minister of police. Quisling complained to Hitler about his exclusion from the government. But the Führer distrusted him; Quisling's desire for an independent Norway clashed with Hitler's long-range intentions to absorb the Nordic country into the Greater German Reich.

During 1941, the failure of Terboven to stem a rising tide of unrest, together with Hitler's fears of a British invasion, prompted the Führer to give Quisling another chance. On February 1, 1942, Terboven made Quisling minister president, theoretically investing him with all the powers formerly held by the king, cabinet, and parliament—while keeping his own sweeping authority as Reichskommissar.

Quisling set out to nazify Norway, focusing on the youth. He established a young people's movement patterned after the Hitler Youth and made membership compulsory for boys and girls between the ages of ten and eighteen. He decreed that all schoolteachers join his party's new Teachers' Front and when faced by widespread refusal, shipped off 500 recalcitrants to a forced labor camp in the Arctic.

Quisling, the traitor, became even more unpopular than Terboven, the Nazi. In September 1942, a special investigator from Himmler's Reich Central Security Office reported that "95 percent of the Norwegian people are anti-Quisling." In fact, the SS had overestimated his appeal. Two months

Josef Terboven, installed as Norway's official German supreme administrator on April 24, 1940, was the second most despised official in the occupation government. Only the Norwegian Vidkun Quisling, the turncoat founder of Norway's Nazi party and later the puppet government's minister president, was more detested.

after Quisling took office, Nasjonal Samling membership peaked at 43,000, or barely 1.5 percent of the population.

The German occupation of the Netherlands bore many similarities to that of Norway. Here, as in Norway, the monarch, Queen Wilhelmina, and her ministers escaped into exile in London; the Dutch "Quisling," Anton Mussert, leader of the local Nazis, hoped to take over as chief of state; and Hitler chose to govern through a civilian Reichskommissar.

To rule the nearly nine million Dutch, Hitler selected one of his own countrymen, Artur Seyss-Inquart. As a member of the Austrian cabinet in 1938, Seyss-Inquart had helped to undermine the Vienna government, paving the way for the Anschluss. Afterward he served briefly as the Reich governor of Austria and then as deputy governor of occupied Poland. He

was a fervent nationalist and believer in the reunion of all Germanic peoples. Nazi theorists claimed the Dutch as close relatives, and Seyss-Inquart considered it his special mission to recover them for Germandom. He was also highly intelligent and by turns amiable and tough; Joseph Goebbels described him as "a master in the art of alternating the carrot and the stick, at putting severe measures through with a light touch."

With Hitler's blessing, Seyss-Inquart began his tenure by offering the carrot. Dutch prisoners of war were permitted to return to civilian life. All political parties except the Marxists were allowed to continue, though the Dutch parliament was suspended. Most important of all, Seyss-Inquart decided to govern through the Dutch secretaries-general, the eleven permanent civil servants who took over the leadership of the ministries for-

Holland's Reichskommissar Artur Seyss-Inquart *(center, in uniform)* briefs members of his occupation government on plans to rebuild Rotterdam, which sustained heavy damage during the German invasion in May 1940. Seyss-Inquart's professed concern for maintaining "the integrity of the kingdom of the Netherlands" soon gave way to an urge to see Holland "brought to a state of obedience."

merly headed by the cabinet members now in exile. He substantially increased their authority but placed them under the supervision of the four German commissioners-general who were his deputies.

At first, Seyss-Inquart studiously ignored the Dutch Nazi movement, known as the Nationaal-Socialistische Beweging (the National Socialist Movement of the Netherlands), or NSB. It was led by its founder, Anton Mussert, a balding, heavyset, square-headed man who liked to strut and posture in the manner of Mussolini. Mussert was an engineer by profession and an unsuccessful politician. Although he was a Nazi, his ardent nationalism had alienated him from Hitler: He opposed the Führer's long-range plan to annex Holland and proposed instead a League of Germanic Peoples led by Hitler but comprising independent nations, including a Greater Netherlands that would include neighboring Belgian Flanders as well as the Dutch and Belgian colonies. Indeed, Mussert and the members of his party spent so much time agitating among the Flemish that the Germans had to close the border with Belgium.

Soon, however, Seyss-Inquart found increasing use for Mussert's party, which doubled its membership to 100,000 during the war. As he began to crack down on the Dutch by banning all political parties except the Nazis and imposing strict radio and newspaper censorship, more and more officials resigned and were replaced by members of the NSB. By 1943, only three of the original eleven secretaries-general remained in office. Local Nazis or their sympathizers filled the vacancies and almost all the important city and provincial posts. Seyss-Inquart even recommended to Hitler late in 1942 that Mussert be named head of the government. It was a trick, the Reichskommissar admitted privately, to make the Dutch people plead for annexation "as a lesser evil." Hitler had a better ploy. He gave Mussert the honorary title "Leader of the Dutch People" and authorized him to form a kind of cabinet known as the Political Secretariat to advise the Reichskommissar. This was largely show, and whatever influence Mussert possessed gradually waned.

A far greater threat to the Reich commissioner's authority came from his own Nazi colleagues. Of all the rival organizations jockeying for power—among them, the office of Göring's Four-Year Plan for the Reich economy, Ribbentrop's Foreign Office, Martin Bormann's Nazi party bureaucracy—none proved more formidable than Himmler's SS. At Himmler's recommendation, Hitler appointed Hanns Albin Rauter as one of Seyss-Inquart's four principal deputies.

As commissioner-general for security, Rauter was theoretically subordinate to Seyss-Inquart. But in his other role, as senior SS officer for the Netherlands, Rauter reported directly to Himmler. Within the loose bounds

of this dual allegiance, Rauter accumulated considerable power. He supervised the Dutch police and all German security forces, with their legions of Dutch undercover agents. He maintained liaison with the Dutch variant of the SS that was organized within Mussert's NSB. He ran the concentration camps and directed all SS troops stationed in the Netherlands, including Dutch recruited for Himmler's military branch, the Waffen-SS. He could even issue arbitrary decrees, such as the one empowering him to take any measure necessary "for the maintenance or restoration of public order and security." Seyss-Inquart submitted to the arrangement, rationalizing his loss of power by claiming that Rauter was merely obeying his own orders. In any event, he admired Himmler and welcomed SS help in Germanizing the Dutch.

Work on this mission proceeded apace. As a step toward integrating the economies of the two countries, currency and customs barriers were eliminated. The Dutch were allowed to apply for German citizenship while maintaining their own. And just as Hitler had done at home, Seyss-Inquart and his SS associates sought to bring together related activities into single organizations that could easily be controlled. Trade unions were transformed into a Netherlands Labor Front modeled after the huge Deutsche Arbeitsfront, or DAF, in Germany. Physicians, artists, journalists, and other professionals were forced into guilds. Such measures worked on paper but proved ineffectual in converting the citizenry. Holland's 30,000 school-teachers were lumped together in one organization, for example, but only 280 were actually Nazis.

To the south, yet a different kind of administration prevailed. For most of the war, a military governor ruled a special administrative zone made up of Belgium and part of northern France. Hitler was uncertain about the future of Belgium. At least for the time being, he decided to join it with the adjacent departments of France—Nord and Pas-de-Calais—and impose military rule. This entire region was strategically critical as a launching area for the planned attack against Britain and as a shield protecting the Reich's vital industrial districts of the Ruhr and the Rhineland.

German rule here proved to be different in tenor as well as in type. The military governor, General Alexander von Falkenhausen, was directly responsible to the army commander in chief rather than to the armed forces high command and the Führer. A Prussian descended from an old Junker family, he was an intellectual who read Stendhal and the teachings of Lao-tsu. He had served in a number of foreign posts: military attaché in Tokyo in 1912, chief of staff of the Turkish army during World War I, representative on missions to Poland during the 1920s, and military adviser

During a summer visit to The Hague in 1942, Reichsführer-SS Heinrich Himmler *(center)* offers advice on antisubversive tactics to a group that includes Reichskommissar Artur Seyss-Inquart *(to Himmler's immediate right)* and the SS police chief Hanns Rauter *(to Himmler's left).* Himmler's adjutant, Karl Otto Wolf, stands stiffly at left.

in China during the 1930s. An opponent of Nazi extremism, he was nonetheless called back from retirement as military governor at age sixty-one, perhaps for family reasons: His uncle had been the German commander in Belgium during the final stages of occupation in World War I.

Belgium, Falkenhausen believed, "could not be ruled with a truncheon." In an effort to avoid encroachments on his power by Nazi functionaries, he exacted obedience from the civilians attached to the military chain of command below him. He brought the industrial economy and agriculture under tight control, merged the free labor unions into a compulsory superunion, and tinkered with the educational system.

His administrative staff was remarkably small. During the summer of 1941, it consisted of no more than 204 officials—a startling contrast to the 10,000 Germans sent into Belgium in 1914. Like Seyss-Inquart in the Netherlands, Falkenhausen relied upon the existing bureaucracy, headed by civil servants who had remained behind when their ministers fled to London to form a government-in-exile. The constitutional monarch, King Leopold III, had chosen to stay on, surrender his army, and enter captivity as a prisoner of war. His hopes of serving the nation under occupation were dashed by Hitler, who ignored him.

Falkenhausen's administration was complicated by Belgium's cultural, political, and linguistic divisions. The population of eight million was nearly split between the French-speaking Walloons and the Flemish, whose language was related to German. Both had their own fascist parties—the Rexists in Wallonia and the Flemish National Union, or VNV, in Flanders. Hitler considered the majority Flemings a Germanic people, and occupation authorities demonstrated this preference with such actions as the early release of Flemish prisoners of war.

It was not long, however, before Hitler began to look with suspicion upon the nationalism of the Flemish VNV, which shared Anton Mussert's vision of a Greater Netherlands. At the same time, the Führer developed a personal admiration for Léon Degrelle, the flamboyant young leader and founder of the Walloon Rexists. "If I had a son," Hitler was said to have remarked, "I would want him to be like Degrelle." Degrelle remodeled his party, which had earlier emulated Mussolini's Fascists, along the lines of national socialism. He also helped organize a brigade of Walloons to fight in the Soviet Union and joined it as a private. By May 1943, Degrelle's influence had helped persuade Hitler that the Walloons, as well as the Flemings, belonged to the Germanic racial brotherhood.

From the beginning of the occupation, Himmler and other Nazi leaders had agitated against Falkenhausen. They rightly asserted that he was lacking in national socialist ardor and clamored for his replacement by a

civil administrator. Falkenhausen was able to limit Himmler's incursion by relying on his own soldiers for police duties instead of on SS security forces.

It was not until July 1944 that Hitler ended the relatively moderate rule of Falkenhausen. At that time, the Führer gave in to Himmler's entreaties and replaced the military governor with a Reichskommissar—Josef Grohé, the gauleiter of Aachen. The transfer of authority took place on July 18, two days before the abortive attempt on Hitler's life. Falkenhausen was suspected of complicity in the plot. He was imprisoned in the concentration camp at Flossenbürg and, in the last days of the Reich, was moved to Dachau, joining Jews and other Belgians his military regime had helped send there. He was at Dachau when the Allies liberated the camp.

The Germans imposed a patchwork of administrative authority on France, which, with its population of 42 million, was the largest of the western countries to feel the heel of the conqueror. The situation in France was unique: For the first two and a half years of the war, a huge chunk of the nation escaped occupation.

The map of France soon after its defeat in June 1940 reflected the hodgepodge patterns of German expediency. First, there were the arrangements at the edges: the two northernmost departments of Nord and Pas-de-Calais attached to the military government in Belgium; the northeastern regions of Alsace and Lorraine all but annexed to the Reich; the tiny southeastern corner ceded to Italy. Then there was the largest chunk, about three-fifths of prewar France: a broad swath across the north encompassing Paris and jutting down the length of the west coast. This was occupied France, governed by the German army. Finally, there was the remaining region in the south, which the Germans left unoccupied for the first half of the war. Known as Vichy France because its capital was the old spa of Vichy about 175 miles south of Paris, this so-called free zone was allowed to maintain its own outwardly sovereign government, France's colonial possessions, an army of 100,000 men, and a navy.

The Germans left southern France unoccupied for several reasons. Doing so enabled Hitler to end the hostilities with France quickly and preserve its Mediterranean fleet, relieving the pressure for it to join up with the British. Allowing part of the country to remain free in name gave the southern French the illusion of independence while saddling them with the burden of administration. Under the armistice agreement of June 22, 1940, the Vichy government not only maintained order in its own zone but also appointed the bureaucracy and supervised the civil administration for both the free zone and the occupied zone. This, of course, helped the Germans by reducing the size of the occupation regime. The occupiers still

retained direct control of the areas of greatest strategic and industrial importance, for these lay in the north.

The very existence of the unoccupied area, moreover, gave the Germans a powerful instrument for manipulating the French in both zones. The line of demarcation that separated the zones represented a serious threat to French economic interdependence. For example, the only factory that made nails for horseshoes was located in Delair in the northern zone; without those nails, all the horses that pulled carts in the south would soon be rendered useless, crippling an important means of Vichy transportation. The occupation authorities could exert pressure on both zones simply by tightening or loosening passage of people and goods crossing the demarcation line. "That line is a bit we have put in the horse's mouth," observed an occupation official, General Karl Heinrich von Stülpnagel, in an appropriate figure of speech. "If France rears, we will tighten the curb. We will loosen it to the extent that France is amenable."

Stülpnagel was one of two cousins, both of them generals, to serve as military governor of the occupied zone. His cousin Otto was the first. As military governor, Otto carried out Hitler's orders for the mass shooting of hostages taken in reprisal for anti-German subversion and also signed anti-Jewish decrees. Karl Heinrich, who succeeded his cousin in March 1942, escaped responsibility for some of the worst repression by insisting on a "clear separation of military and political affairs." In practice, this meant that he surrendered all control over Himmler's SS operatives and their French collaborators, who did the dirty work of deporting Jews and dealing with the Resistance. A secret opponent of the Nazi regime, Karl Heinrich became a key member in the conspiracy against Hitler. On July 20, 1944, the day of the attempt to assassinate the Führer, he ordered the arrest of more than 1,000 Gestapo and SS officers in the occupied zone. After the plot failed, Himmler made certain Stülpnagel went to the gallows.

Germany's relations with Vichy France were often subtle, and evolved mainly through the connection between two men: Pierre Laval, one of the most influential members of the Vichy government, and Otto Abetz, the German ambassador to France. A former high-school art teacher who had married a Frenchwoman and become an expert on France, Abetz occupied a curious position. He was based in Paris instead of in Vichy because part of his job was to advise the military commander on political matters in the occupied zone.

The Vichy administrators required little urging from the Germans to revamp the French government. Convinced that the prewar democratic institutions had been responsible for their nation's debacle, Laval and Marshal Philippe Pétain, the World War I hero of Verdun who had taken

over as French chief of state days before the armistice at age eighty-four, resolved to introduce an authoritarian regime capable of restoring what they regarded as ancient French virtues. On their own initiative, Laval, Pétain, and their colleagues rooted out the parliamentary democracy of the Third Republic. They banned political parties, disbanded trade unions, and excluded Jews from public office and from jobs in education and the mass media. Antidemocratic, anti-Semitic, anti-Marxist, the regime's worst excesses resembled those of Nazi Germany.

The Anglo-American landings in French North Africa in November 1942 forced Hitler's hand. To protect his Mediterranean flank, he ordered the Wehrmacht into the Vichy zone, bringing the remainder of France under military occupation. The pretense of Vichy sovereignty was maintained, but the French soon lost their principal bargaining chips: The North African colonies fell to the Allies and the French fleet was sunk by its own sailors, who scuttled the ships rather than turn them over to the Germans.

The illusion that part of France was still free died. Marshal Pétain, his physical and mental vigor fading, relinquished most of his authority to Laval, who soon found that he had to clear practically everything with the Germans. Because Hitler had designated Vichy France as an operational zone, the collaborationist government now came under the control of the supreme commander for the west, Field Marshal Gerd von Rundstedt. The field marshal's representative, General Alexander von Neubronn, set up shop in Vichy and began assembling a new and cumbersome administrative apparatus separate from the one that already existed for the old occupied zone.

Throughout the years of occupation, long trains and convoys of trucks converged on the Reich laden with booty from the vanquished lands: food for the home front, new weapons for the Wehrmacht, raw materials and workers for the armaments factories, even bullion and currency to finance the war. "The real profiteers of this war are ourselves, and out of it we shall come bursting with fat!" Hitler boasted. "We will give back nothing and will take everything we can make use of."

Responsibility for organizing the pillage of occupied Europe rested initially with Hermann Göring. To oversee the economic exploitation and coordinate the proliferation of Wehrmacht departments, government agencies, and private enterprises competing for the spoils, Hitler empowered Göring to issue orders directly to German occupation authorities. "I intend to plunder," Göring told his subordinates, "and plunder copiously."

Gradually, however, Göring lost ground to competitors. Most of his power in the economic realm was taken over by the efficient technocrats

The Long Arm of the Wehrmacht

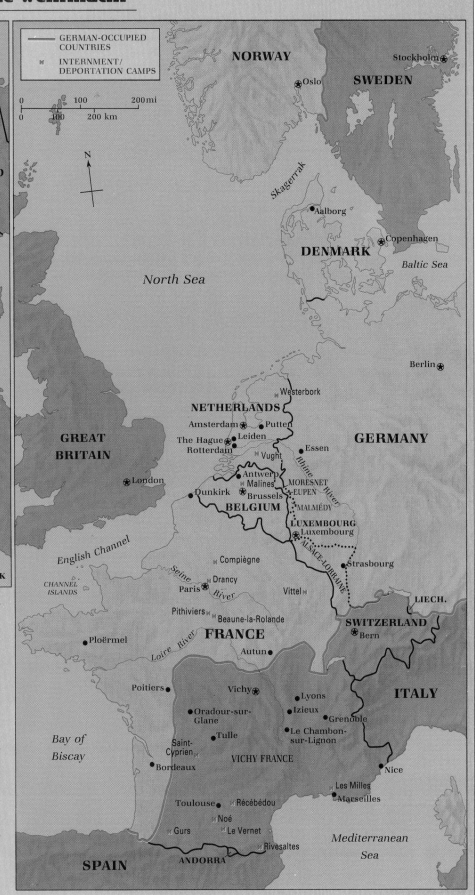

GERMAN-OCCUPIED COUNTRIES

INTERNMENT/ DEPORTATION CAMPS

Beginning in the spring of 1940, Hitler's Wehrmacht forces overran much of western Europe, grabbing territory (*light green*) that included Belgium, the Netherlands, Denmark, and Norway (*above*). In June 1940, the Germans occupied northern France, allowing a puppet regime in Vichy to administer the southern region until November 1942, when they took over the south as well. Not long after seizing these countries, the Nazis established internment camps for resistants, political prisoners, and other "undesirables." Many of the camps became deportation centers from which Jews were shipped to extermination camps in the east.

who headed the Armaments and Munitions Ministry—Fritz Todt, builder of the Autobahn and the West Wall fortifications, and then, after Todt's death in 1942, Albert Speer, Hitler's favorite architect. Göring, meanwhile, more than fulfilled his pledge by pursuing a lucrative personal hobby. He and his agents scoured the galleries of Amsterdam and Paris for paintings by Rembrandt, Rubens, and other masters, amassing through confiscation and bargain purchases a personal collection of art worth hundreds of millions of dollars.

German economic exploitation began with the mere fact of occupation. The vanquished had to pay the victors the costs—as determined by the Reich—of occupying them. France, Belgium, Norway, and the Netherlands were made to pay dearly for resisting the German invasion. Because of their armed defiance, they were officially declared conquered enemy nations. And according to articles from the Hague Convention of 1907, Germany's status as the victorious power gave it certain rights and duties, such as the obligation to preserve order and the right to collect taxes to defray costs of administering occupied lands and supporting their own troops. Armed with this internationally sanctioned authority, the Germans proceeded to drain away their subject countries' resources.

The assessments were astronomically inflated—far in excess of any possible maintenance costs that the army could incur. From 1940 to 1944, the French were made to pay the equivalent of $7 billion annually—ten times the actual costs of the military occupation. Similarly exorbitant fees were levied in the Low Countries. The yearly assessment in Belgium exceeded the annual national budget. And the German occupation cost Norway about 75 percent of its government's yearly income.

The Germans used a variety of stratagems to take control of industry and other enterprises. Frequently, the occupation authorities left factory ownership intact and simply installed their own supervisors to oversee production and distribution. If a factory was owned by a Jew or other "enemy" of the Reich, the Germans confiscated the plant and turned it over to favored industrial combines. The Reich also bought up businesses, using surplus from the payments for the cost of occupation, or even promissory notes that would not come due until after the war and hence had no value if Germany lost. German entrepreneurs also made their own deals. In collaboration with a group of French dye manufacturers, for example, the chemical giant I. G. Farben created a new company called Francolor—retaining majority interest, of course.

Under German prodding, each country was forced to relinquish its resources. Denmark, by delivering butter, cheese, and up to 100,000 tons of meat annually, furnished food for 8.4 million Germans in 1944. Belgium's

Otto Abetz leaves a Versailles

hospital with his wife in August 1941 after visiting Pierre Laval, who was recovering from an assassination attempt.

iron and steel industry supplied 16 percent of the Reich's requirements. Norway's abundance of hydroelectric power was utilized to step up production there of aluminum. The Dutch had one million of their bicycles confiscated by the Wehrmacht, and in December 1942, some 2,300 freight cars laden with toys, cosmetics, and other consumer goods bought cheaply in the Netherlands rolled eastward to brighten Christmas in the bomb-damaged cities of Germany.

No occupied country contributed as much to the German economy as France. From the earliest days of the occupation, when the Wehrmacht loaded 250 freight trains with arms and other matériel and shipped them off to the Reich, France became its largest supplier of food, raw materials, and manufactured goods. Virtually everything made in Vichy France and the occupied zone sustained the German war economy, from wine and grain to aircraft engines and automobiles. In June 1941, one year after the armistice, a French general complained to Marshal Pétain, "The Germans are treating France like a warehouse to be cleared at will."

The Reich was also quick to exploit the manpower of the conquered lands. Some of this resource was claimed by Himmler's Waffen-SS, which recruited 125,000 soldiers in all of occupied western Europe. But it was in the war industries that human labor played the most important role. To begin with, there were the millions of men and women who toiled for the Nazi war machine in their own homelands, frequently under compulsory labor laws that applied everywhere but Denmark. In addition, about four million men and women from the western occupied countries—

A worker off-loads Danish coke, a coal product used for fuel, from a truck onto a German railway car for transport to the Reich. By the war's end, the matériel-poor Germans had seized nearly all of Denmark's meager coal reserves.

Volunteers in the Norwegian Arbeidstjenesten (Labor Service, or AT), instituted by Vidkun Quisling in September 1940, perform road work. A tour of duty in the AT, which Quisling modeled on the Reich Labor Service, was mandatory for all able-bodied young male Norwegians by May 1941.

both prisoners of war and civilians—worked in Germany during the war. During the first two years of occupation, foreigners who worked in the Reich were volunteers. From France came 185,000 workers, from Belgium about 150,000, from the Netherlands some 200,000, from Denmark more than 100,000. They were driven by the unemployment and economic chaos that accompanied defeat at home and by the promise of better jobs and higher pay in the booming industries of Germany, which had lacked a sufficient labor force since prewar days.

By the spring of 1942, volunteers no longer sufficed. The campaign in the Soviet Union was consuming so much manpower and matériel that Hitler decided to replenish his war industries by drafting labor from the occupied countries. To mobilize these workers, he selected Fritz Sauckel, the former gauleiter of Thuringia. A rough-hewn man who admitted he had never read a book, Sauckel promised the Führer to carry out his task with "fanatical devotion"—and did.

Under Hitler's orders, Sauckel could bypass Göring, his nominal chief in the Four-Year Plan, and deal directly with the highest occupation authorities. In western Europe, he concentrated on the three largest countries—the Netherlands, Belgium, and France. He eventually drafted more than 300,000 conscripts from Belgium and Holland. In the summer of 1942, Sauckel decreed a labor draft for occupied France. Meanwhile, he worked out a deal with Laval that would apply to both zones. Under the so-called Relève, or relief scheme, the French government would actively recruit workers; for every three skilled laborers sent to the Reich, Germany would release one of the

Seemingly oblivious to the anti-Semitism that pervaded occupied France in 1942, Parisian children romp inside a park declared off-limits to Jews.

nearly two million French POWs still in captivity. The combination of draft and Relève nearly achieved its goal of a quarter million workers for the second half of 1942, netting some 240,000 Frenchmen. This same quota was met again in the first quarter of 1943, but then recruiting slowed, despite the fact that all of France was now occupied and that Vichy itself had approved a forced labor law.

The labor draft declined, not only in France but elsewhere in occupied Europe, partly because of infighting among the Nazi hierarchy. The Reich armaments minister, Albert Speer, met with success in his ongoing battle with Sauckel. Speer insisted that workers from the western countries could be used more efficiently in war industries at home rather than in the Reich, where they had to be fed, sheltered, and protected from Allied bombing raids. As a result of an agreement concluded between Speer and the Vichy government in late 1943, thousands of French factories with a total labor force of 730,000 were exempted from sending workers to the Reich.

Another deterrent to the forced labor program was the news that filtered to the occupied countries of the increasingly desperate conditions in Germany, where workers were saddled with twelve-hour shifts, cramped barracks, and deductions that took up to 80 percent of their wages. Rather than face involuntary servitude, many French, Dutch, and Belgians fled to the forests and mountains and joined the Resistance.

Sauckel increasingly resorted to draconian methods to meet his quotas. Local police and German agents staged massive roundups, corralling hun-

dreds of men at a time by tactics such as surrounding movie theaters or even churches. In France, his agents shanghaied workers by getting them drunk and then delivering them to recruiting centers. And in an incident in Rotterdam, police and soldiers sealed off the city and rounded up 50,000 Dutch in a single day.

Himmler, in his role as Reich commissioner for the strengthening of Germandom, was the Führer's designated instrument for the racial purification of conquered lands. One of Himmler's fantasies was to transplant thousands of Dutch, with their purportedly superior Germanic blood, onto large tracts of land in eastern Europe to improve the racial stock in that

Gentile residents of Amsterdam promenade outside the barbed-wire boundary of the city's Jewish ghetto, established in February 1941 by the German occupation forces to isolate Jews from the rest of Dutch society.

region. "The orders for initiating this policy," he wrote in 1941, "will be issued after the war."

But he and Hitler had no intention of postponing the realization of their darker fantasy. During the same period when labor conscripts from the west were being sent to Germany, tens of thousands of Jews were sealed in freight cars and moved along the tracks. Occupation authorities said they too were bound for jobs in Germany, but these cars rolled on to death camps in the east. Before the war ended, the gas chambers would claim the lives of more than 200,000 of the estimated half-million Jews living in the western occupied nations at the beginning of the war.

The experience of the Netherlands, which suffered the single greatest loss of Jews in the west, typified the pattern. Almost immediately after the Dutch surrender, Seyss-Inquart and his colleagues applied the twisted racial definition from the infamous Nuremberg Laws—anyone with at least one Jewish grandparent was deemed a Jew—and began confiscating property and businesses owned by those so defined. They expelled Jews from the government and the professions, required them to register with the authorities, forbade them to ride public transport or even bicycles, and forced them to wear the yellow Star of David. They set up a Jewish Council through which prominent Jews would help administer the nightmarish tangle of regulations and paperwork that paved the way to the Holocaust. In September 1941, Himmler's security apparatus established in Amsterdam the final necessary link in the chain of bureaucracy—the Central Office for Jewish Emigration. Less than a year later, in July 1942, this office directed the first large deportations. Of the 110,000 Jews sent eastward from the Netherlands, only 5,000 would survive.

This template of genocide varied according to the circumstances prevailing in each country. In Belgium, the German military government demonstrated little stomach for enforcing Himmler's policies, leaving it up to his own SS agents; about 24,000 Belgian Jews died in the camps. In Norway, Vidkun Quisling paved the way for deportations by reviving a long-dead provision of the constitution that banned Jews and Jesuits from the country; of Norway's 1,800 Jews, 770 were sent to Auschwitz; only 24 survived. In Vichy France, the Pétain government initiated the internment of some 40,000 foreign-born Jews as early as February 1941. From all of France, some 75,000 Jews were deported to the eastern death camps. A mere 2,800 of this number came out alive.

Only in Denmark did the system bog down. Maintaining a light touch with the "model protectorate," the Germans refrained from imposing harsh measures against the over 7,000 Danish Jews for more than three years. Even after Hitler ordered their deportation in September 1943, German

Gendarmes register new arrivals at Pithiviers concentration camp, forty-five miles south of Paris, in May 1941. From Pithiviers and several other holding facilities in occupied France, French Jews were shipped to the death camps of eastern Europe.

officials moved reluctantly. The Reich plenipotentiary, Werner Best, is said to have indirectly leaked word of the impending arrests and forbidden the police to enter Jewish homes. With the help of their countrymen, all but about 480 escaped to Sweden.

Nor did the Danes forget those whom the Germans had managed to find. Danish officials kept pestering the occupation authorities about the welfare of these people, most of whom had been too old to hide or escape. They sent food and clothing and even made visits of inspection to Theresienstadt camp in Czechoslovakia, where the Danes were being held. Their extraordinary efforts helped thwart the Nazi death machinery and achieved a record unique among the occupied nations: So far as is known, not a single Jew from Denmark perished in the gas chambers.

The French at Work for the Reich

To the Nazis, the nation of France, with the largest number of skilled workers in occupied Europe, was the answer to Germany's critical labor shortages.

Eager to improve upon the production being forced out of its million prisoners of war, the Reich waged an intensive campaign to recruit French workers, at first offering the same enticements given workers in Axis and neutral countries. Propaganda campaigns initiated by the Reich Labor Ministry promised high salaries, good living conditions, sixty-hour workweeks, and short-term contracts. Married workers were guaranteed a vacation every three months and were allowed to send home up to 250 reichsmarks per month. Unmarried workers were promised a vacation every six months and could send back 150 reichsmarks each month. Among other inducements, the Germans also claimed that French and other western European workers would receive the same working conditions, food rations, fringe benefits, and housing as their German counterparts.

The recruitment campaign was enhanced by economic strictures imposed by the occupiers. The Nazis prohibited salary or price increases in France and hauled away huge amounts of French consumer items for use in Germany. The remaining goods inevitably ended up on the black market, where prices were often too high for the fixed wages of the French people. When faced with economic deprivation, a French worker tended to be more receptive to the prospect of a German factory job.

Initially, at least, the recruiting campaign worked. As of October 1, 1941, more than 48,000 French men and women had been persuaded to accept jobs at factories and farms in Germany. But it was not long before disillusionment set in as the workers realized that the Germans were not fulfilling their promises.

French volunteer workers in Berlin, recruits in Germany's labor

With a shield on his arm and a hammer in his hand, the French worker in this labor recruitment poster fends off the Russian bear. "By working for Europe," the caption reads, "you protect your country and your home."

OUVRIER!

EN TRAVAILLANT POUR L'EUROPE
TU PROTÈGES TON PAYS ET TON FOYER

campaign, deposit a wreath at the city's Tomb of the Unknown Soldier in November 1941.

VOUS AVEZ LA CLEF DES CAMPS

travailleurs français
**VOUS LIBEREZ LES PRISONNIERS
EN TRAVAILLANT EN ALLEMAGNE**

"You have the key to the [POW] camps," this Relève poster says. "French workers: Free the prisoners by working in Germany." Premier Pierre Laval, executed at the end of the war for treason, told his countrymen that it was their patriotic duty to participate in the Relève program.

In this propaganda photo, beaming volunteers wait to sign up for Relève, the program that would place them in German factories.

Minister of Production Jean Bichelonne (*second from right*) visits a Relève training center.

A Nazi Demand for "Volunteers"

By early 1942, the stream of French volunteers had dwindled to a trickle, and it was clear to the Germans that stronger measures would have to be taken to satisfy the Reich's labor requirements.

Fritz Sauckel, Hitler's minister of labor, demanded that France increase its exported labor force to 250,000 by the end of July or face a draft. In response Pierre Laval, the premier of Vichy France, proposed the Relève, a voluntary system that appealed to French patriotism by guaranteeing the release of one French prisoner of war for every three workers sent to Germany.

Relève proved to be a huge failure. Only 31,300 new workers had been recruited by July, and in compliance with Sauckel's demand, the French government enacted a compulsory labor law. By the beginning of 1943, German organizers had taken control of the draft effort, and French factory workers were being dragooned from their assembly lines and sent to Germany. In June and July, 116,000 new workers were forcibly dispatched to Germany.

Sauckel's flow of workers came to a virtual standstill, however, when Albert Speer, the Nazi minister of war production, began exempting workers in French factories that were manufacturing goods for the German war machine. By autumn, thousands of French factories were classified as "S-plants," their workers immune to Sauckel's labor draft.

Grateful French POWs *(far right),* freed by the Relève program, return from Germany in a train that bears the inscription, "Our hearts know no hate." The recruiting poster *(inset)* depicts a stream of prisoners making their way home while laborers—such as the French metalworker pictured below—march cheerfully off to Germany.

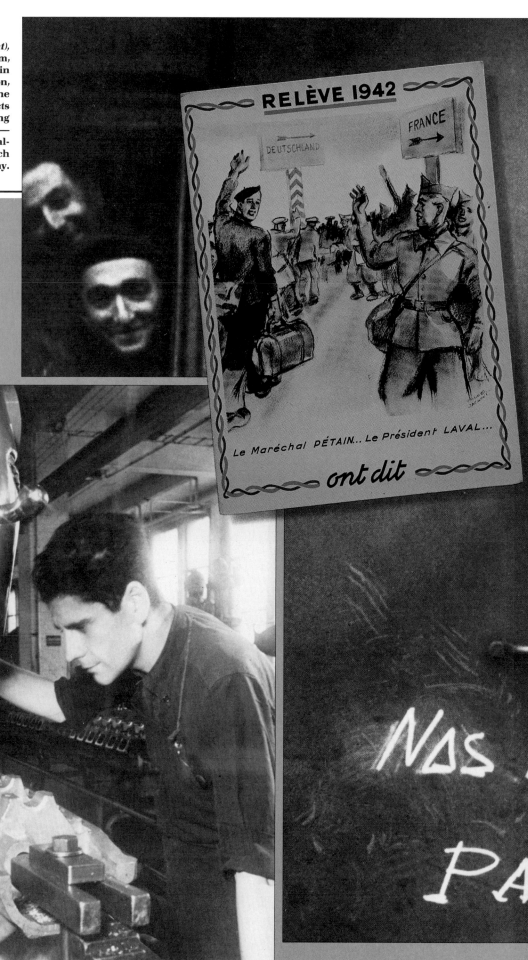

RELÈVE 1942

DEUTSCHLAND

FRANCE

Le Maréchal PÉTAIN... Le Président LAVAL...

ont dit

Young Frenchmen eligible for conscription report to the Paris Census Bureau to register.

The Manhunt for Reluctant Laborers

In January of 1944 Fritz Sauckel, ordered by Hitler to harvest a million more French laborers during the year, was forced to take drastic measures to meet the quota. All French males between the ages of sixteen and sixty and all women between eighteen and forty-five were ordered to register for the labor draft. Sauckel then organized armed cadres of French police and turned them loose to hunt down labor draft violators, who were jailed in France or sent as prisoners to work in Germany.

Still hamstrung by Speer's S-plant exemptions, Sauckel took the further step of decreeing that a payment of up to fifty reichsmarks would be offered as a reward to any French person who turned in a countryman to the labor draft.

Thousands of eligible French workers chose to join the Resistance and disappear underground rather than submit to virtual slavery in Germany. In addition, cooperation from French officials was at best sluggish, and Sauckel continued to be frustrated in his effort to fulfill Hitler's demand.

On June 6, the Allies invaded Normandy, effectively ending Nazi labor recruitment in France. Sauckel had managed to procure fewer than 30,000 French workers in 1944, a far cry from the million he had promised Hitler.

Drafted workers in Paris wait for

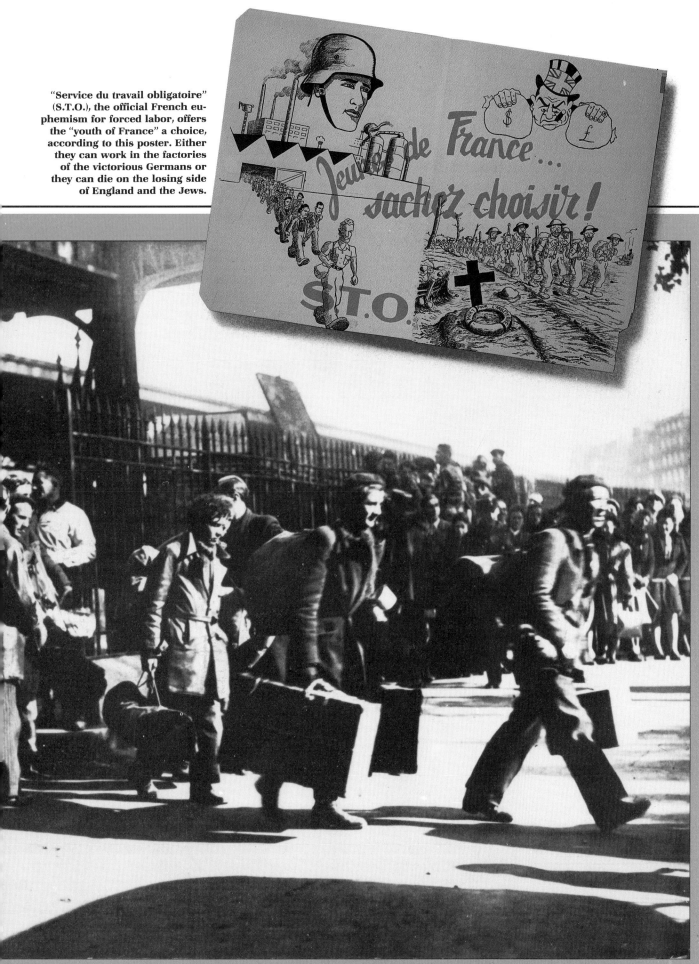

"Service du travail obligatoire" (S.T.O.), the official French euphemism for forced labor, offers the "youth of France" a choice, according to this poster. Either they can work in the factories of the victorious Germans or they can die on the losing side of England and the Jews.

Jeunes de France... sachez choisir!

S.T.O.

trains that will carry them to Germany, where they will stay for at least two years.

REVOLUTION
NATIONALE

TWO

The Stain of Collaboration

ess than six months after the capitulation of France, on November 28, 1940, the Chamber of Deputies of the French National Assembly gathered in Vichy to hear the Nazi ideologue Alfred Rosenberg interpret their nation's defeat. "The decadent successors of the French Revolution have clashed with the first troops of the great German Revolution," Hitler's unofficial philosopher proclaimed. "With that, this era of 1789 is now approaching its end. In a triumphal victory it was crushed when, already rotten, it still arrogantly attempted to go on dominating the destiny of Europe in the twentieth century as well." Many of the disillusioned legislators agreed with Rosenberg's historical assessment. They saw France's collapse not only as proof of the impotency of the Third Republic (the government formed in 1870 after the fall of Napoleon III) but also as a signal of the approaching death of democracy itself. Was national socialism the wave of the future? All across the Continent, citizens of the conquered lands asked themselves that question as they attempted to come to grips with their defeat.

Everyone faced the same stark choice: to collaborate with the Germans or resist them. There was no middle ground. The rewards of resistance were intangible and remote, the dangers concrete and immediate: Anyone caught defying the Germans was in immediate peril of imprisonment or execution. Collaboration, on the other hand, offered not only survival but the possibility of gaining concessions and a return to normal life. Other considerations, too, operated to deter one from taking a courageous stand against the invader.

Unlike in Poland, where the Germans dealt brutally with the citizenry, the occupying forces in the west were on their best behavior, and the peace terms seemed relatively mild. Hitler insisted that he only wished to protect the neutrality of Scandinavia and the Low Countries; and his armistice with France, while harsh, was not dishonorable.

Furthermore, most Europeans assumed that the war was all but over and that Germany had won. Although they mistrusted and resented the Germans, many of them directed their wrath against their own monarchs and

The visage of the aged Marshal Philippe Pétain, president of France and collaborator with the Germans, stares from a 1940 poster issued by his anti-democratic Vichy government. Pétain's "National Revolution" urged a return to what he called France's "ancient virtues" of work, discipline, and obedience.

governments who had fled into exile. Their sense of abandonment was heightened by appeals from their former leaders for further resistance when it seemed clear that a continuation of the conflict would only magnify the catastrophe. No one wanted a repetition of the First World War.

Not surprisingly, the vast majority of Danes, Norwegians, Dutch, French, Belgians, and Luxembourgers were far more ready to cooperate with the Germans than to oppose them. But whatever their motivation—fear, expediency, the desire to preserve social order, hopelessness in the face of German might, belief in national socialism, or simply an inclination to conform—any hopes they might have had for gaining an advantage were never realized. Hitler had no intention of granting privileges or power to anyone—even to puppet politicians, such as Vidkun Quisling in Norway or Anton Mussert in the Netherlands. Although he naturally turned to Nazi sympathizers for help in administering his new empire, Hitler viewed collaborators of every stripe with suspicion and cynicism. "If they act against the interests of their own people, they are dishonorable," he once said. "If they try to help their people, they become dangerous." To Hitler, the conquered peoples had value only to the extent that they aided his war machine and supported his racial policies.

Late in the war, the term *collaborator* developed a treasonous connotation. In fact, virtually everybody who lived through the war in the occupied lands compromised himself to some degree. The philosopher Jean-Paul Sartre, who published his major philosophical work, *Being and Nothingness*, during the German occupation, and eventually joined the French underground, spelled out the dilemma: "We could not stir an inch, eat or even breathe without becoming the accomplices of our enemy. Not a drop of blood formed in our veins, but he took his share of it. The whole country both resisted and collaborated. Everything we did was equivocal; we never quite knew whether we were doing right or doing wrong; a subtle poison corrupted even our best actions."

In all the occupied countries, national and local bureaucracies chose to stay at their posts, continuing to perform their daily functions, rather than walk out in protest of the invasion. A strike, civil authorities reasoned, would only open the door to more intrusion by the Germans into day-to-day life and increase the hardship on the community at large, which still needed utilities, fire departments, transportation facilities, hospitals, and other public services regardless of the German presence.

This administrative continuity occurred more or less automatically in Norway, Denmark, Luxembourg, and France. The governments of Holland and Belgium, however, ordered their civil servants to cooperate with the

Traders throng the floor of the Paris stock exchange on the day it reopened, October 8, 1940, four months after the fall of France. By then many Parisians who fled the German onslaught had returned to the city, shops were open, and life was outwardly back to normal.

Germans, so long as the occupier did not force them to act against the national interest. As early as 1937, in fact, both countries had prepared guidelines spelling out the responsibilities of public officials in the face of an enemy invasion. In Belgium, railroad and power-station employees were expected not only to fulfill their duties but to give assurances to the occupiers that they would commit no sabotage. In Holland, a proviso for a similar collaboration was that the Germans not impose a Nazi government on the Dutch people.

Although the occupied could collaborate with the Germans while silently loathing them, it was not uncommon for friendships to develop. German railway engineers, medical officers, and military policemen naturally sought out their foreign professional counterparts. Romances flourished too, especially in France, even though German soldiers were not allowed to marry citizens of occupied countries. Still, by the middle of 1943,

in the Vichy zone alone, 80,000 Frenchwomen submitted claims for children's benefits to the German military authorities and requested German nationality for their offspring.

Marshal Philippe Pétain, the Vichy chief of state, first announced his government's stance toward Germany after a meeting with Hitler in the Führer's private railroad train at the French town of Montoire in October 1940. He told the French people in a radio broadcast, "I have today entered the way of collaboration." Instead of a "traditional peace of oppression," he said, France and Germany were embarking on an "entirely novel peace of collaboration."

But the old marshal never intended collaboration to mean servility or treason. With the war lost, as he judged it to be, he believed that it was his duty—and that of every true patriot—to make the best possible accommodation for France. His expectation was that in time France, through its superior culture, would become a "brilliant second" to Germany within Hitler's new European order.

The Nazis, however, had no intention of granting France a favored status.

Pétain and Hitler shake hands after agreeing on a policy of French collaboration during a meeting in the Führer's railroad car at the station of Montoire in October 1940. The interpreter, Paul Schmidt (*center*), recalled that Pétain dealt with Hitler imperiously, like "a marshal talking to a corporal."

The German communiqué detailing the meeting between Hitler and Pétain made no reference to Franco-German collaboration, and Joseph Goebbels, the Reich minister of propaganda, ordered the German press not to mention it. Hitler himself used the term only once, in a letter to Pétain in November of 1942, after he had violated the terms of the armistice by ordering German troops to occupy the Vichy zone: As a cynical courtesy, the Führer informed Pétain that he hoped to chat with him about closer Franco-German ties.

From the beginning, Hitler had only scorn for the French—and especially for the collaborationists. According to Goebbels, Hitler's willingness to listen to talk of collaboration was intended "only for the moment." Goebbels later confided to his diary: "If the French knew what demands the Führer will one day make on them, their eyes would probably pop. That is why it is better to keep mum about such things for the present." Before he would even consider concessions, Hitler expected the French to prove their loyalty by deeds.

For his part, Pétain did his utmost to prevent France from becoming a mere German satellite. The proud old marshal dug in his heels at demands that he considered excessive or dishonorable. He declined Hitler's proposal that France join in the war against Great Britain and evaded Nazi orders to turn over airfields and

A placard circulated by the extreme right wing in France expresses disappointment in the results of the Montoire meeting. By failing to collaborate sufficiently, it says, Pétain was encouraging the Jews and endangering Franco-German relations.

other installations in the French colonies. He also refused to disarm the French fleet or allow French merchant ships to carry supplies to German forces in North Africa.

Even as Pétain was parrying Hitler's demands, other elements in Vichy were organizing secret-intelligence services to look out for France's long-term interest. These included the Bureau for Antinational Subversive Activities, or BMA, a counterespionage center in Marseilles, and an organization called Firme Technica, which was a front for counterespionage operations. In the first year of the occupation, these undercover organi-

zations arrested hundreds of Axis agents and executed many of them.

Soon, however, Vichy's determination to salvage a measure of French independence eroded, and no one was more responsible for this than Pierre Laval, the influential deputy in Pétain's cabinet. A shabby, sallow-skinned, baggy-eyed little man, Laval was a career politician and a skilled negotiator. First elected to office in 1914 as a Socialist deputy, he won the premiership several times in the period following World War I, and attained a number of lesser cabinet posts as well.

Over the years, Laval had grown frustrated with France's parliamentary system, which, he believed, was producing only demagoguery and inaction in the face of dire national problems. Convinced that democracy was leading the nation to ruin, he angled his political views to the right. In the 1930s, he studied the ways of Mussolini and later became an outspoken advocate of appeasing both Mussolini and Hitler. His defeat in the 1936 elections left him embittered and even more determined to reform the French constitution.

Laval got the opportunity in July 1940, during debate by France's elected representatives over adopting a new form of government under Marshal Pétain. Before the debate began, Laval boasted to a colleague: "The parliament vomited me up. Now I shall vomit it up."

"Since parliamentary democracy wished to enter into a struggle with nazism and fascism, and since it lost that struggle, it must disappear," he told the assembled parliamentarians. "A new regime—one that is bold, authoritarian, social, and national—must take its place."

Laval's arguments carried extra weight as a result of the surprise British naval attack on the French fleet on July 3 as it lay at anchor off the coast of Algeria at Mers-el-Kebir. The British, fearing that the French ships would be seized by the Axis powers, shelled the fleet, sinking one battleship, disabling two others, and killing 1,300 French sailors. From the Vichy perspective, the British action was outrageous because France had pledged to keep the fleet out of the war. A furious Laval accused the British of having first led France into disaster and of now exploiting the French to save their own skins—an argument many Frenchmen agreed with.

Laval saw himself as saving France through a reconciliation with Germany. "I don't believe in the permanence or even the long life of nazism," he once said. "In fifteen or twenty years' time, Europe will have a new thirst for freedom. If the French flame has been kept alight, albeit dimly, it is to her that they will come to rekindle the extinguished torches, for there will be no one else."

When the French representatives voted to abolish the National Assembly and grant Pétain authoritarian powers, the marshal appointed Laval to the

post of vice premier. It was not long before Pétain became disillusioned with his deputy, however, and in December 1940, he risked Hitler's wrath by dismissing Laval from his cabinet—largely because of Laval's intrigues to promote outright military collaboration. The dismissal only confirmed Hitler's distrust of the nation he had labeled in *Mein Kampf* as "the German people's irreconcilable mortal enemy."

Over the passing months, under increasing German pressure, Vichy began yielding the very concessions that Pétain at first had refused to make. In March 1941, Admiral Jean-François Darlan asked for and received German permission to use French warships to protect French merchantmen from the British fleet. The following month, Pétain agreed to let the Luftwaffe use French airfields in Syria. He also acceded to a request that the German navy be allowed to supply the Afrikakorps from the French-controlled port of Bizerte in Tunisia, and he made the harbor at Dakar, along with other military installations in French West Africa, available for German use. Hitler's meager response was to return a few captured torpedo boats, temporarily reduce occupation fees, and release some 75,000 French prisoners of war.

At Hitler's demand, Pétain resurrected Pierre Laval in April of 1942, naming him chief of government. From then on, Pétain's influence began to recede, and Laval became the main instrument of German power in France. Pushed ceaselessly to yield to ever-increasing demands, Laval gave the Germans just what they wanted. He disbanded the Vichy intelligence services and allowed plain-clothes German security police to enter the unoccupied zone and hunt down French resistants. He looked the other way as the Germans whisked away their victims to concentration camps inside the Reich. At the same time, Laval stepped up Vichy's own police actions. In October of 1942, Vichy police captured more than 5,000 French Communists, some 400 members of the Resistance, and forty tons of hidden weapons. General Karl Heinrich von Stülpnagel, the German military commander in France, praised Laval for a job well done. The ultimate humiliation came one month later when the Wehrmacht marched into the Vichy zone in blatant violation of the armistice.

As Goebbels had predicted in 1940, the French had no idea how destructive collaboration eventually would be. Laval seemed to acknowledge the extent of the disaster in early 1943. The occasion was a request from Fritz Sauckel, Hitler's slave-labor recruiter, for another 250,000 French workers. Laval retorted: "I represent a country that has no army, no navy, no empire, and no more gold. I represent a country that still has 1,200,000 prisoners of war in Germany, while 900,000 of its workers, whether in Germany or in France, in the last resort, work for Germany." On the French

On December 19, 1942, Laval
(below), then the Vichy premier,
is harangued by Reich Marshal
Hermann Göring on a visit to
Wolfsschanze, Hitler's military
headquarters in East Prussia.

side, Laval said, it was all sacrifice; on the German side, all coercion.

And so it continued until the liberation in 1944. Laval and Pétain could only feebly acquiesce as the Germans increased their demands for economic help and took harsher action against the growing French Resistance.

Beginning in 1943, the hapless leaders of the Vichy government were compelled to sanction a campaign of terror against the Resistance launched by the French members of the Milice française, a paramilitary force of 45,000 volunteers led by the Frenchman Émile Joseph Darnand.

Darnand was a passionate nationalist and a man of action. In World War I, he was awarded one of France's highest military honors, the Médaille militaire, which he received from Pétain himself. Between the wars, he joined a succession of right-wing extremist groups, including the dread Cagoule (Monk's Cloak), a secret society dedicated to fighting any Communist threat to the French government by any and every means, even a coup d'état. He rejoined the army and fought again against the Germans in the spring of 1940. After the armistice, Darnand moved to the Vichy zone to run the Nice branch of the Légion des combattants (Legion of War Veterans), an organization formed by Pétain to support Vichy policies.

Restless for action, he created the Service d'ordre légionnaire, or Legion Police Force, as a Vichy praetorian guard. From this group the Milice would be formed. The legionnaires swore an oath of loyalty to Pétain and to France and vowed to fight against the Communists, the Jews, freemasonry, and Charles de Gaulle, the Free French leader in London exile.

After the Allied occupation of North Africa, Hitler began to fear a possible invasion of the French Mediterranean coast. Worried about partisan attacks against his army's rear, he summoned Laval and demanded that he organize an auxiliary police force to keep order. Laval complied, approving the establishment of the Milice on January 31, 1943, with himself as its president and Darnand as its secretary-general.

Laval expected the Milice simply to protect Vichy's interests, but Darnand turned it into a French SS. The Germans rewarded him with the rank of major in the Waffen-SS, and he outfitted his men in a style similar to that of the Nazi Storm Troopers, with a khaki shirt, black tie, dark blue pants and jacket, and a beret. The Germans provided their weapons.

By late spring of 1943, the Milice was engaged in a bitter fratricidal war with the Resistance. The bloodletting continued until the arrival of the Allied armies the following summer. Darnand sought refuge in Germany, then fled into northern Italy where elements of the Milice were fighting Italian anti-Fascists. He was captured and transported back to France for trial, where he refused to defend himself. Sentenced to death, he was shot by a firing squad.

After the war, Laval and Pétain were tried for treason by a high court of justice set up by Charles de Gaulle's provisional government. Both Vichy leaders were sentenced to death. Out of respect for Pétain's advanced age and his stature as a World War I hero, de Gaulle commuted the marshal's punishment to life imprisonment. He lived out his days in quiet exile in the fortress on Île d'Yeu, south of the Brittany peninsula, dying in 1951 at age ninety-five. To his final breath, Pétain insisted that he had acted in the nation's best interests. "The French people will never forget," he claimed, "that I saved them at Vichy as I had saved them at Verdun."

Laval met a stormier fate. His trial took place in an atmosphere of poisonous recrimination and had scarcely begun before Laval accused the prosecution of not allowing him to defend himself. He boycotted the remainder of the hearings.

Kept in chains in the condemned block of Fresnes prison outside Paris, Laval tried to cheat the firing squad by swallowing poison from a secret vial that he had carried with him throughout the war. But the poison, which was too old, failed to kill him. The former French premier was revived and then half carried to the execution stake, tormented by thirst. His widow

Organizer and head of the Milice, Vichy France's fascist police, Émile Joseph Darnand (*center*) attends a 1944 assembly with a leather-coated bodyguard on one side and a Milice officer in uniform and beret on the other. Pierre Laval once observed that the rough and ruthless Darnand possessed "about as much political intelligence as a curbstone."

defended him to the end. "It is not the French way to try a man without letting him speak," she complained. "That is the way he always fought against—the German way."

Elsewhere in occupied Europe, the prospect of collaboration was welcomed by a collection of would-be Hitlers who hoped to achieve high office. For his part, Hitler looked foward to receiving help from these like-minded ideologues in spreading the seeds of nazism and building the German New Order in Europe. As it happened, however, Hitler and the European national socialist leaders would prove to be a great disappointment to each other. The Führer hoped to find native Nazi leaders with large public followings and a willingness to serve as figureheads in puppet governments controlled by Berlin. Instead, he encountered a sorry collection of inept politicians with small constituencies and grandiose dreams of glory.

One of these pretenders, Vidkun Quisling, got off on the wrong foot with Hitler with his botched attempt to take over the Norwegian government during the German invasion in April 1940. The farcical coup, which Quisling explained as an attempt to reach "an understanding with our Germanic fellow race" and win for Norway "a leading position in the working of the New Order," embarrassed the Nazis and gained Quisling worldwide notoriety. Not only did the Norwegian civil service refuse to obey his orders, even his chosen ministers from his own National Assembly party failed to support him. Most damaging of all, the German ambassador to Oslo rejected him as unfit to rule, despite instructions from Hitler to help establish a Quisling-run regime.

The Norwegian Nazi shared some character traits with Hitler, without possessing any of the Führer's ruthlessness or political cunning. Like Hitler, Quisling had a powerful sense of his own destiny. He was convinced that he had been born to lead Norway to new heights. He was fond of pointing out that his birthday, July 18, 1887, coincided with the anniversary of the battle of Havsfjord, at which Harald Fairhair defeated the other Viking kings and emerged the ruler of a united Norway. The son of a Lutheran pastor and distantly related to the great Norwegian playwright Henrik Ibsen, Quisling grew up enormously proud of his ancestry. "I was brought up among Viking graves, amidst scriptural history and the sagas," he once said. "I belonged to an ancient house, and I was inculcated with a belief in family pride, family history, and our responsibility to our people. The name *Quisling* is no foreign name, but an ancient Nordic name. Q is not an outlandish Latin letter, but an ancient protective rune."

Quisling intended that his National Assembly party, which at first he called Nordic Awakening, unite Norwegians from all walks of life in a solid national bloc. "Our party will not be a party in the same sense as the other parties, but a party beyond party, an organized revival," he claimed. "In it farmers, workers, and burghers will be able to find a part to play in the national task." In Quisling's theoretical society, all decisons for the Norwegian people would be made by an authoritarian elite, led by him, who understood their needs better than they did themselves.

Whereas Pierre Laval saw England as the ultimate enemy of a new European order, Quisling was anxious for Germany to make peace with the British. He worried that a bloody war would do irredeemable damage to the Nordic race and spoil his vision of a "Greater Nordic Peace Union." British obstinacy forced him to change his mind, however, and he came to the conclusion that Britain had become too contaminated by Jewish blood to be redeemed.

Quisling's rampant anti-Semitism was wildly out of place in Norway, where Jews had enjoyed full rights of citizenship since 1851. By 1940, they were fully assimilated into Norwegian society and virtually indistinguishable from the rest of the population. Quisling developed his prejudice in the 1920s when he was working with a League of Nations team providing famine relief in the Soviet Union. His original enthusiasm for communism had turned to hatred at the sight of the starving Russian peasants, victims of Stalin's brutal repression. Like so many others in central and eastern Europe, Quisling found scapegoats in the Bolshevists and the Jews. He blamed the Jewish and partly Jewish members of the Communist party

The Norwegian fascist Vidkun Quisling, protected by German SS soldiers and his own storm troopers, strides toward Oslo's parliament building, where he was installed as the figurehead prime minister of Norway on February 1, 1942.

hierarchy for polluting the ideals of the 1917 revolution. He accepted at face value the *Protocols of the Elders of Zion,* the notorious Russian forgery that purported to be an authentic report of a secret Jewish congress aimed at destroying Christian civilization.

Although Quisling's beliefs never attracted more than a small band of followers in Norway, he stubbornly refused to compromise them. His anti-Semitism did, however, win him powerful support in high Nazi circles. The Nazi party's chief ideologue, Alfred Rosenberg, became his mentor and patron. It was Rosenberg who interceded with Hitler to appoint Quisling minister president in 1942, over the bitter objections of Reichskommissar Josef Terboven. But Quisling's concept of Norway as an independent partner did not suit Hitler's plans. Although the Führer was still unsure how he would eventually govern Norway, he was adamant that it would become part of the Reich.

During his puppet regime, Quisling willingly acquiesced in the persecution of his fellow citizens, especially Norway's Jews. History has judged him to be the quintessential collaborator. In fact, that role in Norway was played to an even greater extent by his younger rival and minister of police, Jonas Lie, who actually carried out the dirty work.

Lie was a hardheaded Nazi quite unencumbered by Quisling's muddleheaded idealism and obsession with racial theory. He had been friends with Terboven since 1934, when the future Reichskommissar for Norway was gauleiter of Essen and Lie the head of a League of Nations team assigned to oversee the Saar plebiscite. Soon after the occupation began, Lie became a protégé of Heinrich Himmler, who sent him to the Balkans for SS training. In Norway in the summer of 1942, he was given command of the Germanske Norge SS, a police unit, and proceeded to terrorize his fellow citizens. Lie was just as hard on his own policemen. Once when an underling disputed an order, Lie arrested him, along with 470 of his fellow officers, and shipped them all off to a German concentration camp.

After the war, in May of 1945, Lie committed suicide. Quisling, stubborn and unrealistic to the end, attempted to negotiate a transfer of power with representatives of the Norwegian Resistance. Not about to grant terms of surrender to the man almost all Norwegians considered a traitor, the Resistance representatives arrested him. After the government-in-exile returned to Oslo, Quisling went on trial, charged with a long list of offenses from embezzlement of public funds to high treason.

Since Norway had no death penalty in its civil code, the government tried him under military law. He was found guilty and sentenced to death; in order to execute him legally, however, the Norwegian Supreme Court had to waive a clause that specified that the death penalty could be enacted only during actual hostilities. Quisling wrote a letter to King Haakon protesting the illegality of his trial, but refused to appeal for mercy. He spent his final hours reading the Bible. On October 24, 1945, he was taken to the old Akershus Castle in Oslo, then blindfolded and shot. His last request had been to shake hands with the firing squad.

The experience with Quisling taught Hitler a lesson about the pitfalls of trusting foreign sympathizers. When informed that Anton Mussert, the leader of the National Socialist Movement of the Netherlands (NSB), was a nationalist with ideas of his own about the makeup of a new European order, Hitler might have discarded him out of hand had he not needed Mussert's party to fill bureaucratic posts and carry out such tasks as confiscating Dutch property and enforcing Sauckel's labor drafts. Realizing that Mussert would never desert the German cause no matter how he was treated, Hitler denied his plea for the creation of a Greater Netherlands

Flanked by flag bearers, Holland's chief Nazi, Anton Mussert, addresses the Dutch National Socialist party's annual meeting in Amsterdam in 1941 wearing his usual Mussolini-style black shirt. Mussert proved woefully ineffectual as the "Führer of the Dutch people," a role Hitler allowed him to play.

The Dutch fascist Rost van Tonningen is married in a 1940 civil ceremony to one of his female followers, who wears a fascist symbol on her necklace. Rost van Tonningen was a rival of Anton Mussert for primacy in Holland's Nazi-style National Socialist party.

Reich with himself as chief executive. If Mussert were the actual head of state, Hitler reasoned, the unpopular measures that had to be taken to Germanize the Dutch would undermine Mussert's authority with his own people. Instead, Hitler inserted Mussert into Holland's occupation government, making him an adviser to Reichskommissar Artur Seyss-Inquart.

Mussert's efforts to get the Führer to accept the idea of postwar Dutch independence also failed. Hitler refused to commit himself. By way of argument, he drew a parallel between the Dutch reluctance to join the Reich and the unwillingness of some German states to join Bismarck's Prussian-dominated Reich in 1871. Hitler claimed that he had been willing to do away with the independence of his own native Austria for the sake of the Greater German Reich. He expected no less from Mussert.

Seyss-Inquart used Mussert's NSB to help govern the Netherlands much as Terboven used Quisling's National Assembly party in Norway—as a source of ideologically acceptable manpower. In time, more than half of Holland's mayors and 70 percent of the provincial commissioners were NSB men. Many other Dutch Nazis held lesser bureaucratic posts.

The more ambitious of the Dutch collaborators vied hotly for recognition and power. Seyss-Inquart's favorite among them was not Mussert, whom he criticized as being "essentially nationalistic, not national socialist," but one M. M. Rost van Tonningen, the head of a radical faction of the NSB and a rival of Mussert. Rost van Tonningen won the Reichskommissar's approval for being "perfectly adequate" ideologically and "adjusted to the Germanic idea." So in tune with Nazi dogma was Rost van Tonningen that, unlike Mussert, he advocated Holland's complete Germanization, including the introduction of the German language, German culture, and German institutions. And he had nothing but scorn for Mussert's nationalism. In founding the NSB, Mussert had evoked Holland's history, especially the seventeenth-century golden age when Dutch navigators crisscrossed the globe, bringing home enormous wealth. He had made *"Houzee!"* (Hold steady!), the cry of the Dutch sailors during the struggle for independence

from Spain, the official party greeting. Such attempts to foster Dutch national pride were frowned upon, not only by Rost van Tonningen but also by the German overlords.

Influenced by hard-line Nazis like Rost van Tonningen, the puppet Dutch government grew more and more compliant in the hands of the Nazi overlords. Dutch officials acquiesced when Seyss-Inquart barred Jewish students and faculty from Dutch universities, and when he closed down the University of Leiden for failing to comply. The Dutch Nazi Jan van Dam, secretary-general of the new Department of Education, Science, and Protection of Culture, ordered the Germanization of curricula and imprisoned any teacher who failed to cooperate. In late 1942, van Dam asked the university rectors to give him a list of 7,000 students who could be sent to work in Germany. When all but one refused, the Germans allowed van Dam to drop the plan. Thousands of lesser NSB members became agents and informers for the Gestapo. Although Mussert's original NSB policy favored freedom of religion and rejected anti-Semitism, NSB members and the Dutch police joined with the Gestapo and the Security Police in rounding up Holland's Jewish community.

In the end, of course, the most ardent and vocal of the collaborationists in Holland paid the ultimate price, as they did elsewhere. After the liberation, Mussert and Rost van Tonningen were arrested by Dutch authorities. Mussert was convicted of treason and hanged in The Hague on May 7, 1946. Rost van Tonningen escaped trial by committing suicide.

Danish collaborator Fritz Clausen is portrayed as a jumping jack—whose strings are pulled by the Germans—in a cardboard toy distributed by a rival fascist in Denmark. The box of coffee with its Jewish name implied that Clausen was also a tool of the Jews. The sausage in his hand suggested that he was profiting from the war.

Denmark's leading Nazi, Fritz Clausen, a physician from the province of Schleswig, was a firm Germanophile. The structure of the party that he founded in the 1930s, the Danish National Socialist Labor party, was an exact copy of Hitler's Nazi party, with entire sections of its program translated word for word from the German. Clausen's storm troopers, the Storm-Afdelingr, wore brown uniforms like the SA, and the party anthem was nearly identical to the "Horst Wessel Song," the German Nazi anthem.

Clausen wanted nothing so badly as to be recognized by the Führer as a dedicated collaborator, and he zealously lobbied to be appointed

The elaborate funeral cortege of Belgian fascist leader Staf de Clercq (*inset*), who died in October 1942, passes by government buildings in Brussels as ranks of his followers in the Vlaamsch National Verbond party dutifully give the Nazi salute.

premier of Denmark. At first Hitler intended to make use of Clausen as a successor to King Christian. But when the Führer realized how small Clausen's party was, and how unpopular it was with the Danish people, he abandoned the notion.

Yearning for success, Clausen appealed so frequently to the Reich plenipotentiary to Denmark, Cecil von Renthe-Fink, for a share of power that Renthe-Fink came to regard him as a pest and a source of friction. Clausen tried to impress the German overlords by waging a campaign to mobilize wealthy Danish landowners and industrialists to push for closer relations with Germany. In 1942 he even tried to carry out a coup d'état against the Danish occupation government, sending his Brown Shirts into the streets of Copenhagen to brawl with the Danish police. But to his chagrin, Hitler continued to ignore him.

Clausen, like his counterparts in western Europe, came to an ignominious end. In 1943 he gave up his quest for power and volunteered for the Waffen-SS. But instead of earning glory on the eastern front, he ended up in a German hospital, suffering from alcoholism. He died of a heart attack while awaiting trial for treason in a Danish prison.

In Belgium, two forceful personalities, representing the two main fascist parties, vied vigorously for Hitler's favor and their share of power in the hierarchy of the occupation. Staf de Clercq, head of the Flemish National Union party (Vlaamsch National Verbond), or VNV, was a former teacher and a member of the Belgian parliament whose devotion to Nazi ideals was so ardent that he and his Flemish followers promised to be ideal collaborators. But like many of their fascist counterparts elsewhere in Europe, de Clercq and his successor, Dr. Hendrick Elias—de Clercq died of natural causes in 1942—were tarred in Hitler's eyes by the brush of nationalism. And like Mussert in Holland, the two men were obsessed with the creation of a Greater Netherlands, including the Netherlands, Belgian Flanders, French Flanders, and the Dutch and Belgian colonies. They defended Flemish national aspirations so tenaciously that Hitler was compelled to abandon his idea of using VNV members to help the occupation regime Germanize the Flemish population.

The rival Rexist party, which represented the French-speaking Walloons, eventually proved more valuable to the Germans, thanks to its dynamic leader, Léon Degrelle. The youthful and vigorous Degrelle founded the party in 1935, appealing to Wallonia's patriotic, royalist, and religious sentiment. (The name *Rexist* was derived from the Latin phrase *Christus Rex.*) Drawing its support largely from the nobility, the industrialists, and the high-ranking military, the Rexist platform called for the merger of the

Outfitting the Auxiliary SS

After opening their ranks to non-Germans, Waffen-SS officials pondered the question of how to clothe the thousands of recruits who showed up to fight dressed in everything from civilian garb to paramilitary uniforms. Standard attire was needed, but the Nazis felt ideologically compelled to distinguish these foreigners from the inherently "superior" German SS. Allowing each foreign unit to wear its national army uniform would mark the newcomers as non-Germans. But such a practice would lead to chaos on the battlefield and would violate international law; the Allies could execute SS troops caught wearing uniforms of nations that were technically Germany's enemies. The solution: standard SS uniforms embellished with national insignia.

Although non-Germans were eligible for the same medals awarded to German troops, some collaborationist regimes created special military decorations for their citizens who fought with the Nazis. Vidkun Quisling's Norwegian government struck a medal depicting a Viking warrior *(top)*. In the Netherlands, Anton Mussert devised his own award for bravery, the Mussert Cross *(bottom)*. Though most foreign SS units had their own awards for excellence in sports and military exercises, the Nazis replaced these in 1943 with the German Proficiency Badge *(middle)*.

To identify their nationality, most non-German soldiers in some foreign contingents of the Waffen-SS wore distinctive arm shields with national or regional colors and symbols *(below)*. From left to right, the shields represent Denmark, Norway, the Netherlands, France, Dutch-speaking Flanders in northern Belgium, and French-speaking Wallonia in southern Belgium.

Foreign SS troops often displayed national names or regional designations on their cuff titles, the black band a soldier wore on his left coat sleeve to identify his unit. This tunic belonged to a second lieutenant serving with an artillery battalion in the SS Standarte Nordland, or Nordland Regiment, a unit of Norwegian and Danish volunteers. Pinned to the left breast pocket are an Iron Cross and a Wound Badge.

Flanked by his young son and daughter, Léon Degrelle strikes a heroic pose at a fascist rally in Brussels in 1944. Degrelle, a pious Catholic, derived the name of his fascist Rex movement from the Latin term *Christus Rex*, "Christ the King."

Flemings and the Walloons into a single national party modeled on nazism. The first time Degrelle offered the support of his party to the German occupiers, however, he was turned aside. Nazi racial theorists, including Himmler, viewed the French-speaking Walloons as racially unsuitable partners. But Degrelle's willingness to organize a Walloon SS unit to fight alongside the Germans on the Russian front helped to establish his credentials. No less valuable was his continued insistence that Wallonia had deep Germanic roots and that he and his followers supported Hitler wholeheartedly in his drive to unite the greater Germanic community.

Himmler remained a skeptic until the spring of 1943 when he inspected Degrelle's military unit, which had become a part of the Waffen-SS as the Germanic Volunteer Legion. Himmler came away impressed by the Nazi ardor of the young Walloons. The Wehrmacht was suffering increasing losses in the east, fresh fighters were essential, and consequently the racial theories of both Himmler and Hitler were becoming less rigid. Hitler now referred to Degrelle's volunteers as "the renaissance movement of a basically Germanic people." The Walloons and the Flemings were now prepared, the Führer decided, "for a very clever and delicately managed future process of amalgamation."

Of the original unit of 850 Walloons who volunteered to fight against the Red Army, only 3, counting Degrelle, survived. But Hitler never rewarded Degrelle with a political post. Although some Rexists and VNV members worked in the occupation administration of General Alexander von Fal-

kenhausen, the Belgian fascists were deemed most useful to the Germans as soldiers in the service of the Wehrmacht.

Degrelle escaped to Spain after the war. A Belgium high court tried him for treason *in absentia* and sentenced him to death, but he was able to elude the law. Decades after the war, Degrelle remained unrepentant about his collaboration with the Germans. In an interview with Dutch journalists in

Slogging through mud on the eastern front in February 1945, Léon Degrelle leads the retreat of his Walloon SS volunteer brigade, which he organized after the German invasion of the Soviet Union.

1973, he called Hitler the greatest statesman of his age and added, "I am only sorry I did not succeed, but if I had the chance, I would do it all again—much more forcefully."

France had more than its share of collaborators who scorned Vichy but had little else in common except the desire to take advantage of the German presence to push their personal ambitions. Both of the leaders of France's two largest fascist parties, Marcel Déat and Jacques Doriot, began their careers as leftists: Doriot as a Communist, Déat as a Socialist.

Doriot, born into a working-class family and trained as a metalworker, was tall, powerfully built, and charismatic, with a gift for public speaking. In 1923 he was selected by French Communists to attend the Party School in Moscow for training as a Communist organizer, a move that launched his career. In 1924, he won a seat in the French Chamber of Deputies, and later was also elected mayor of the Paris suburb of Saint-Denis. His followers hailed him as the Red Crown Prince. But he fell from Communist grace when, in defiance of directives from the Comintern, he supported a united Socialist-Communist front in France, for which act he was expelled

New recruits sign up at an office of the Parti populaire français, or PPF, in July 1941, beneath a poster of the party's demagogic leader, Jacques Doriot. The PPF was the largest fascist organization in France, with 130,000 members by the outbreak of war.

from the party. In 1936, he founded his own right-wing party, the Parti populaire français, or PPF, and began drawing huge crowds to the Vélodrome d'Hiver and other Paris gathering places with his violent speeches against Communists, capitalists, and Jews. By March 1937 the PPF had its own flag, anthem, Nazi-style salute—and 130,000 members.

Doriot's new organization caught the eye of high-ranking Nazis. But, as was his practice elsewhere, Hitler intended to string the French fascists along, using them for his purposes but denying them any significant role in occupation government, or in the formation of the new Europe that lay ahead. The Germans gave Doriot no position of power, nor did they provide arms for the paramilitary forces that he had formed. They were, however, willing to enlist his aid occasionally in pressuring the Vichy government

Parisian journalist and publisher Jean Luchaire received generous payments from the German occupiers in exchange for the pro-Nazi views he espoused in print. Luchaire used the funds to support a lavish lifestyle.

to yield to their demands. In the fall of 1941, Doriot helped Déat recruit a Légion des volontaires français contre le bolchevisme (French Anti-Bolshevist Volunteer Legion), or LVF, for service on the Russian front, and served there himself for eighteen months. He also cooperated with the Gestapo in the suppression of the French Resistance. But it all came to nothing in the end—in February 1945, Doriot was killed in an aircraft-strafing attack near Mengen, Germany.

Mastermind and chief torturer of the French branch of the Gestapo, Henri Lafont (*left*) stands trial after the war along with Pierre Bonny (*in glasses*), a former police inspector who helped Lafont organize his deadly campaigns against Jews and the French Resistance.

Marcel Déat, head of the other pro-Nazi party in France, was cut from different cloth than Doriot. He was an intellectual who at twenty-six became a professor of philosophy at Paris's prestigious École normale supérieure. In 1926, he won a Socialist seat in the Chamber of Deputies, but gradually his political thinking took a turn to the right. Déat came to believe that the only way to achieve a just society was through a fascist dictatorship: What France needed was a strongman, like Hitler. Certainly the French did not need to fight against Germany, a point Déat argued in an article entitled "Die for Danzig?" published when Germany was pressuring Poland to yield that Baltic port city. Shortly after the Wehrmacht overran France, Déat formed his party, the Rassemblement national populaire, to lead the glorious "march into fascism." As with the other national fascists, Déat expected his collaborationist efforts to earn him a key position in the French Nazi government that he assumed would replace Vichy after the war. He wanted to be a leader so badly, one of his enemies wrote, "he will be one in German if he cannot be one in French."

Pétain appointed Déat a minister of labor in the Vichy government and allowed him to join Jacques Doriot in forming the LVF. But that was all. The Germans had about as much respect for Déat and Doriot as the Wehrmacht had for the legionnaires that the two French fascists had mustered. Of the 13,400 initial recruits in the LVF, only 3,000 were passed by German doctors

as fit for duty. The rest were rejected for such deficiencies as bad teeth, varicose veins, or poor eyesight. Total enrollment as late as May 1943 was only 6,400. When the legionnaires arrrived at their training camp in Poland, they were required to swear allegiance to Hitler and forced to exchange their French uniforms for German field gray.

France had other enthusiastic collaborators, many of them motivated as much by greed as by ideology. The most opportunistic of them was the tall, handsome, debonair Jean Luchaire, proprietor of the newspaper *Notre Temps*. For a fee, Luchaire would print articles on any issue. Throughout the late 1930s, the Germans regularly paid him to publish their propaganda, and *Notre Temps* became filled with stories aimed at undermining the French will to resist. During the occupation, the publication sang the praises of Hitler's New Order, and Luchaire became a wealthy man.

Far more sinister than Luchaire was Henri Chamberlin, a large, muscular man with an incongruously high-pitched voice, who went by the alias Henri Lafont. Born in the Paris slums, Lafont blossomed as a career criminal. He was in prison in 1940 when the German armies poured into France, and he took advantage of the resulting confusion to escape.

Back in Paris, Lafont found work procuring meat and vegetables— sometimes by force or theft—for German intelligence personnel. The Germans shielded him from the French police, who sought to put him back where he belonged, in prison. Recognizing his ruthless qualities, the Germans decided to send Lafont on a more important errand—to track down a Belgian Resistance leader named Lambrecht who was reported to have taken refuge in the Vichy zone. Lafont ran Lambrecht to ground in Toulouse. Bursting into the Belgian's room, he subdued his victim and thrust him into the trunk of a waiting car for delivery to Gestapo headquarters in Bordeaux. There Lafont helped the Germans interrogate Lambrecht about his Resistance network, wrenching from him information that led to the arrest of more than 600 of the organization's members.

Lafont's feat earned him a promotion. By early 1941 he was ensconced in a branch Gestapo headquarters at 93, rue Lauriston, an elegant house in a wealthy section of Paris. From there he recruited a gang of unscrupulous compatriots who posed as German policemen to extort money from wealthy Parisians by threatening them with arrest. Lafont and his men terrorized their victims into handing over any valuables they might still possess, and then divided up the booty with the Gestapo. With his extorted wealth, he became a prominent figure in Paris society, often attending the Longchamp races and throwing lavish parties.

Lafont's more lethal specialty, however, continued to be the infiltration of Resistance networks. Over the years, he betrayed and killed hundreds

The Amsterdam Jewish Council, an organization created by the Nazis that was made up largely of prominent scholars and

businessmen from the city's ancient Jewish community, meets to deliberate policy in November 1942.

of his own countrymen. If on his missions he came across any Jews in hiding, he turned them over to the Germans as well. So ruthless was Lafont in his treachery that many patriotic Frenchmen considered him more dangerous than the Gestapo itself.

After the liberation, Lafont was captured on a farm east of Paris. Some members of his gang escaped, but he and a number of his closest associates were tried and executed by a firing squad in December 1944. The Lafont gang, however, represented only a small portion of the French collaborators willing to spy on their fellow citizens. According to German records, some 32,000 French agents worked for the Gestapo during the occupation. Most of them escaped justice, melting back into the postwar population.

Of all the varieties of collaboration practiced in western Europe, perhaps the most tragic was that cooperation innocently undertaken by what were known as Joodsche Raad, or Jewish Councils—special bodies of Jewish leaders who volunteered to represent their communities in their dealings with the Nazis. The Germans first used the system inside the Reich, later honed it in their satellite states and conquered lands in the east, and finally used it to devastating effect in Belgium, France, and the Netherlands. Some of the most distinguished Jewish leaders cooperated, thinking that they might be able to protect the Jewish population, or at least make life easier for a few. As the council leaders saw it, they were doing the best they could to maintain the life of their community at a time of terrible crisis. Council duties included administering Jewish bank accounts, issuing travel and resettlement permits, distributing food and medical care. In the Netherlands, the council also published a newspaper, *Het Joodsche Weekblad*, that contained stories, editorials, advertisements, and notices of weddings and births. It also printed directives and threats handed down by the German government for distribution.

The Dutch council did the Germans' paperwork for them, compiling lists of Jewish names and addresses and keeping them up-to-date. The cruel system helped the Germans camouflage their true intentions. German orders were transmitted by the council, which gave them a legitimacy they would otherwise have lacked. Many Jews believed when they were deported that they were going to labor camps in the east, as they had been told, instead of to death camps. The council even transmitted deportation orders and helped the Germans round up the deportees. Ultimately, the council was forced to designate its own employees for deportation. At the end, many of its own leaders went east to their deaths as well. Of the 140,000 Dutch Jews who registered in the 1941 enrollment, about 110,000 were deported. All but 5,000 perished in the extermination camps. ✚

Foreign Legions for the Reich

In the summer of 1940, after years of vying with the Wehrmacht for the cream of German manhood, the head of the SS, Heinrich Himmler, turned to the newly occupied nations of Norway, Denmark, Holland, and Belgium for recruits for his Waffen-SS. For Himmler, these Nordic volunteers not only would plug a manpower gap but also would become part of a racially superior army that would lay the foundation for a pure Aryan Europe. In his recruitment drive, Himmler appealed to nationalist instincts, promising that foreign volunteers would join their countrymen in forming SS regiments that would represent the occupied nations. What he did not emphasize was that German SS officers would command the regiments, and that within them, German SS rules would apply.

Himmler's invitation was not warmly received. Most eligible young men in the occupied countries felt no ideological kinship with the SS. Of those who did volunteer, the majority signed up for practical reasons. For men trapped in economical hard times, the Nazis offered immediate relief in the form of good food, smart uniforms, and adventure; SS promises of government jobs and land when the fighting was over seemed to guarantee a bright future.

Despite these enticements, recruitment continued to fall far short of expectations. It picked up only after Germany invaded the Soviet Union in July 1941. Europeans who despised Hitler found themselves searching for a way to fight what they regarded as an even greater menace, communism. To tap this pool of patriots, Himmler concocted the notion of foreign legions, national armies that purportedly would be independent of the SS. Thousands answered the call. But the concept of national armies proved to be short-lived. Although some recruits were trained and led by their countrymen, by 1943 the SS had dropped all pretense of allowing independence, disbanding the legions and reassigning the volunteers to German as well as to foreign Waffen-SS units. Most of the non-German units, small and lightly armed, were decimated on the battlefields of the eastern front.

Declaring that "the same kinds of blood fight together against the same enemy," the poster above urges Norwegians, Danes, Dutch, and Flemings to join the Waffen-SS. Foreign volunteers wore cuff titles *(below)* bearing the names of their units.

Norway's Nazi Soldiers

In June 1940, the SS began a recruitment drive in Oslo for a new regiment called Nordland, a unit for Norwegians and Danes. Himmler combined the handful of men who joined with two other regiments: a German one, Germania, and Westland, whose members were Dutch or Flemish. When Germany attacked Russia in 1941, this new creation, called the Wiking Division, went to battle in the Ukraine.

To attract more fighters, Himmler created a national Norwegian legion. Rumors that it would be sent to defend Norway's longtime ally Finland from the Soviets helped to swell the legion's ranks. In March 1943, after fighting near Leningrad for a year, the force was combined with a Danish legion and the Nordland Regiment to form the Nordland Division. This group and the Wiking Division were among six non-German units that futilely struggled to block the Soviet advance at Narva in Estonia in July 1944. Both divisions suffered heavy losses, but each one limped on to more tough battles in the east. At the war's end in 1945, Nordland's men were among the last defenders of Berlin, while the Wiking Division surrendered near Salzburg, Austria.

In Oslo in 1942, a Norwegian SS company comprising mostly former policemen proudly displays its new flag before leaving for Leningrad *(right)*. **In the snowy wilderness north of Leningrad in 1944, weary Norwegians clad in winter camouflage huddle around their tiny fire for warmth and coffee** *(inset).*

German troops protect the Freikorps Danmark as it marches through Copenhagen in September 1942.

In April 1944, men from the Nordland Division's SS regiment Danmark slog through trenches along the Narva River (right).

The Free Corps from Denmark

The SS recruiting poster above appeals to Danish pride by comparing the 1944 Narva conflict with the Danish triumph there in 1219.

From the time the SS arrived in Denmark in April 1940 until the following February, only 200 Danes signed up for the Nordland Regiment. After Hitler's invasion of Russia, however, the Danish government formed a legion that boasted more than 1,000 men by the end of 1941. From its inception, the force was really run by the Waffen-SS, a fact that was kept hidden. The legion's very name, Freikorps Danmark, was a German-Danish hybrid. After a year on the eastern front, the unit was withdrawn from active duty in 1943 and transformed into the SS regiment Danmark. As part of the Nordland Division, the Danes fought at Narva in 1944.

Dutch SS volunteers swear allegiance to Hitler in The Hague in October 1941. The Nazis drew many recruits from Holland's multitude of right-wing political and paramilitary organizations.

Dutch SS troops haul a gun into place at Leningrad in April 1943. The Netherlands contributed almost as many volunteers to the Waffen-SS as all the other Nordic countries combined.

Dutchmen in the Waffen-SS

When the Nazis occupied the Low Countries in 1940, a thousand men, Dutch and Flemish, signed up for the new SS regiment Westland. Impressed by this response, the Nazis then created a second regiment, Nordwest. After the invasion of Russia, the SS attached Westland to the Wiking Division in the Ukraine.

Most of Nordwest's Dutch recruits were assigned to the newly created Freiwilligen Legion Niederlande, or Volunteer Legion Netherlands. The unit fought mostly in northern Russia but moved south in the war's final days; as the 23d SS Panzer-Grenadier Division Nederland, it surrendered in May 1945.

Resplendent in black uniforms, the Black Brigade, a Flemish right-wing militia that supplied the SS with manpower, stands at attention during a July 1942 ceremony in Brussels.

The weary face of a begrimed Flemish soldier *(left)* shows the strain of the trench warfare on the Leningrad front in 1942.

The Belgian Regiments

In Belgium, the SS dismissed the French-speaking Walloons as inferior and signed up 1,200 Flemings for the regiments Westland and Nordwest. Later Himmler organized a legion, Freiwilligen Legion Flandern, around the Flemings from Nordwest. In November 1941, the legion was shipped to the front, where it was repeatedly battered before being pulled from the line in May 1943. Reinforced, the Flemings returned to the front in December as the 6th SS Volunteer Assault Brigade Langemarck. This Belgian brigade, along with the Walloons, who had been allowed to join in 1943, was annihilated by the Soviets near the Pomeranian town of Stettin on April 19, 1945.

THREE

The Pulse of Resistance

What happened in Denmark puzzled the Germans. Suddenly, in the period following Denmark's capitulation, the defeated Danes started singing. There were only a few score of singers at first. In a rural Jutland township, a baker and a schoolteacher thought to invite some friends and neighbors to a communal songfest at one of their homes. The word went around, and so many people arrived that they all had to crowd outside, where their voices filled the street with the echoing strains of popular ditties, folk melodies, and hymns. In the weeks to come, more and more Danes started to sing, until one Sunday in September, after France had collapsed and while Adolf Hitler's legions were goose-stepping through Paris, 150,000 Danes gathered to raise their voices in Copenhagen's Faelled Park, and hundreds of thousands more turned out to sing in cities and towns throughout the land. All told, 2,000,000 people, two-thirds of the entire population, joined in song that September evening.

Wisely, neither the occupiers nor their collaborators attempted to interfere. By then, of course, the Germans understood the import of the singing. It was one of many such gestures the occupiers were encountering: a subtle act of resistance, a reaffirmation of national identity, of pride and self, of enduring hope and an unquenchable human spirit. Yet this was a time when the Germans still envisioned Denmark as a "model protectorate," and expected that the rest of western Europe would acknowledge German suzerainty and acquiesce to German demands.

In this they were mistaken. Civilian resistance began almost from the moment of surrender, and with Allied support it would gain momentum as Germany's military fortunes declined. At first it was modest and largely symbolic. But then it grew more bold, taking the form of labor strikes and outpourings from the underground press. Simultaneously, networks of Resistance members focused on aiding fugitives from the Germans. Finally, there was massive espionage and sabotage, and in the late stages of the war, resistance from what were, in effect, "home armies"—aggregations of thou-

Captured French Resistance fighters, the "maquis," march off under the guns of German-supported French fascist militia in Ploërmel, Brittany, on June 2, 1944. More maquis were executed as a result of being betrayed than died fighting the Germans in the formative years of the Resistance.

sands of men who at times would engage the Wehrmacht in pitched battle.

The Germans responded by mounting a counterresistance strategy that was sophisticated, thorough, and relentless. Directed by men experienced in security, it relied heavily on informers, random raids, advanced technology, and classic police surveillance. The security forces imposed curfews and censored mail, banned strikes and street demonstrations, restricted movement, and purged the personnel of local newspapers and radio stations. At the same time, the Germans sought to infiltrate and control schools, labor unions, the medical and legal professions, churches, and civic associations.

The antiresistance campaign commenced with persuasion and propaganda, but when that failed the Germans had to fall back on a complex apparatus that was an extension of the security forces in the Reich: the army's bureau of military intelligence, or Abwehr, together with two branches of the SS, the Secret Police, or Gestapo, and the Security Service, or SD. In addition, there were the Order Police, a paramilitary force charged with carrying out arrests, mass raids, deportations, strikebreaking, and executions. The Germans established kangaroo courts staffed entirely with these police, acting as prosecutors, witnesses, judges, jurors, and even as spokesmen for the defense. Finally, to maintain daily order, the Germans relied on existing local police forces that were amenable to supervision.

Yet for all their efficiency, the Germans never had sufficient means to control an area of more than 375,000 square miles, with a population greater than 70 million. So increasingly, as resistance stiffened, the occupier resorted to terror, intending to drive the cost of defiance so high that the occupied peoples would be unwilling to pay it. The terror claimed tens, possibly hundreds of thousands of victims. No one can be sure of the number. But in the long run, terror fueled the very opposition it was supposed to stamp out, and resistance in western Europe was far stronger by the time of the Allied invasion than ever before.

At the beginning of the occupation, the conquered peoples expressed their determination to prevail in gestures both large and small. In Holland, men waiting at street corners removed their hats and stood at attention when the traffic signal shifted to orange, a mute tribute to the House of Orange and their exiled queen. The carnation was known to be Norway's King Haakon VII's favorite flower, and so on his birthday, August 3, thousands of Norwegians carried carnations and scrawled the inscription "H7" on walls and signs throughout the land. For their part, loyal Danes wore badges emblazoned with their King Christian's royal monogram in silver and enamel, along with lapel pins formed of the letters *SDU* (for *"Smid dem*

ut"—"Chuck them out"), while teenagers distributed a paraphrase of the Ten Commandments ("Thou shalt not trade with the Nazis," etc.) on the streets of Copenhagen. All over occupied Europe, people stubbornly planted flower beds in their national colors, and wore caps and clothes made to look like flags. Meanwhile, they offered small insults to the Germans: Citizens pointedly waited until German newsreels had ended before entering movie houses, refused to look German soldiers in the face, pretended not to understand a word of German even when they spoke it fluently.

The Germans for the most part shrugged off these early snubs and provocations. Occasionally, however, they reacted. In Oslo, bus-stop signs went up announcing that to change places "when one finds oneself sitting beside a German" would be regarded as a hostile act. And the Dutch got a taste of German wrath the very first time they organized a real display of symbolic resistance, seven weeks after the country's surrender. The Germans had forbidden the singing of the national anthem and the showing of the national colors. But crowds ignored both prohibitions as they marched to the Royal Palace in The Hague on Prince Bernhard's birthday to sign the birthday register. To teach the Dutch a lesson, the Germans arrested General H. G. Winkelman, former commander in chief of the Dutch army, and hauled him off to a concentration camp. But it was in France where the shape of the future was most clearly drawn. On November 11, 1940, a thousand students marched down the Champs-Élysées singing the "Marseillaise" in celebration of Armistice Day and the German surrender in World War I. The Germans were enraged. Ninety students were arrested, and an engineer being held in a military prison on a totally unrelated charge was executed—just as a warning.

A German SS officer looks on smugly as a Danish policeman dutifully arrests a woman sporting a cap in the shape and color of the roundel, the insignia of the British Royal Air Force. A popular symbol of support for the Allies, the red, white, and blue caps were outlawed in Denmark in 1943.

What especially galled the Germans were growing signs of resistance within professional groups that they had hoped to dominate. The Dutch triggered German fury when the occupiers set out to gain control of the

medical profession by installing their own man in a key post of the Netherlands Medical Association. Member physicians responded by resigning and forming their own clandestine association, the Medical Contact. When the Germans established an officially sanctioned State Medical Chamber and insisted that all Dutch doctors join it, more than 6,000 physicians announced that they were ceasing practice. The subsequent arrest of 360 doctors only caused others to disappear into the underground.

German efforts to establish control over the churches, the labor unions, and the educational systems met similar rebuffs. The Norwegian church flatly rejected the Nazi puppet Vidkun Quisling in an escalating confrontation that Quisling could not win. The Nazis hoped to enlist church support in a "crusade against bolshevism," and upon Quisling's assumption of power on February 1, 1942, one of the few Norwegian clerics with German sympathies attempted to hold a special celebratory service in the cathedral at Trondheim. No one attended; everyone waited for the regular service conducted by the dean that afternoon, and then they jammed the cathedral and, in defiance of a police ban, spilled outside to stand in the cold singing "A Mighty Fortress Is Our God." The dean was immediately ousted from his post, and in protest, every bishop resigned along with virtually all the pastors. The clergy continued to perform their duties at small, private gatherings, but the church pulpits and pews were empty, and Norway had no established church from then on until the end of the war.

Similar confrontations were played out in every conquered country, where the churches threw the full weight of protest against anti-Jewish measures, forced labor, random imprisonment, and other cruel features of German rule. Not even the arrest of hundreds of Dutch Protestant and Roman Catholic ministers and priests—and the execution of ninety-two of them—could bend the churches to the Nazi will; they forbade membership in the Dutch Nazi party and denied the sacraments to those who already belonged. Nor could the arrest of French priests halt the Catholic Church's steady movement away from the Vichy government and toward the aims of the Resistance, which many priests joined.

Against dissident teachers and students the Germans took a hard line right from the start. They correctly perceived the schools as prime breeding grounds for resistance. In Belgium, Holland, and France, recalcitrant universities were shut down "for anti-German activities"—often meaning a refusal to swear allegiance to the Third Reich—and teachers and students were conscripted for forced labor. And when Norwegian teachers refused to join a German-sponsored union, the authorities shipped off 1,000 offenders to concentration camps, while packing another 500 aboard a dangerously overloaded coastal steamer for transport to labor gangs in the far

Helmuth von Moltke, German hero of the Resistance, carried this passport with him when he traveled to Oslo to free Bishop Eivind Berggrav. Before his execution for treason in January 1945, Moltke wrote, "Ever since national socialism came to power, I have tried to ease its results for its victims and to prepare the way for change."

The Wehrmacht's Secret Samaritans

On April 8, 1942, the Third Reich's puppet regime in Norway, led by Prime Minister Vidkun Quisling, cracked down on the nation's un-cooperative clergy by arresting their leader, Bishop Eivind Berg-grav, primate of the Norwegian Lutheran Church and a central fig-ure in the Norwegian Resistance movement. Quisling intended to have Berggrav condemned to death by a fascist kangaroo court, but his plans were thwarted by interven-tion from an unexpected source— the Germans themselves.

This remarkable turn of events was brought about by Lieut. Colo-nel Theodor Steltzer, a fifty-seven-year-old World War I veteran and staff officer at the headquarters of General Nikolaus von Falkenhorst's occupation army. Unknown to his military colleagues, Steltzer was a member of a Resistance group in Germany centered around Count Helmuth James von Moltke, a legal adviser in the Abwehr, the armed forces intelligence agency.

Steltzer had been in secret com-munication with the Norwegian underground since his arrival in Oslo in August 1940. He passed on valuable information about im-pending Gestapo actions and used his influence to lighten sentences imposed on political prisoners, or to help Jews and other endangered Norwegians escape.

On the day of the bishop's arrest, Steltzer telegraphed Moltke in Ber-lin. Moltke appealed directly to his boss, Admiral Wilhelm Canaris, the director of the Abwehr and also a clandestine member of the anti-Hitler movement.

Canaris arranged for Moltke to go to Oslo. There he and Steltzer, ar-guing that punishing Norway's leading cleric would only increase local unrest and thus was not in the best "interests of the Wehrmacht," managed to persuade the occupa-tion authorities to cancel the pro-ceedings and release Bishop Berg-grav from prison.

Although Berggrav remained un-der house arrest in Oslo until the end of the war, sympathetic Nor-wegian policemen enforced the confinement loosely. Dressed in disguises, he was able to sneak away regularly to attend Resistance meetings in the city.

After the war, the Norwegians honored Lieutenant Colonel Theodor Steltzer *(left)* by making him the first German to be presented to their restored monarch, King Haakon VII.

After his release from prison, Eivind Berggrav, shown in his clerical garb *(below)*, and tilling his garden under the eye of police guards *(opposite, top)*, adopted various disguises to circumvent house arrest. He posed as an Oslo policeman, and in mufti wearing glasses and a fake mustache *(opposite, bottom)*.

north. Adolf Hitler, on hearing that the German crew of this vessel had issued life jackets to the teachers, deplored this "orgy of German good nature." The teachers, he snorted, should be "delighted to be torpedoed by their beloved Britishers and sent to the bottom."

Trade unions, however, were regarded favorably by the authorities, at least in the beginning. The Germans and their homegrown Nazi acolytes saw the labor movement as a perfect platform for spreading German political ideas to a broad audience. Consequently, early in the game, when both Communist and non-Communist unions in Holland and Norway dissolved themselves rather than submit to German domination, the occupation forces dropped most of their demands, fearing a general strike.

Yet strikes there would be—in endless, debilitating profusion, and they proved to be among the most successful psychological weapons of resistance. Untold millions of workers engaged in them, demonstrating that resistance was possible and encouraging other forms of revolt. German efforts to suppress the strikes were only intermittently successful.

The first general Dutch strike against German rule occurred in Amsterdam in early 1941. In response to hostile acts against the city's Jewish population by the Dutch Nazi party, people emptied office buildings and factories and brought public transportation to a standstill. The Germans opened fire on the demonstrators, killing 11 of them; 4 strike leaders were executed, and 1,000 other strikers were rounded up and deported.

Although this show of force quelled further demonstrations in Amsterdam, strikes continued to erupt elsewhere in the country. In 1943, after the Germans ordered all former Dutch soldiers to report for reinternment in Germany, workers in the industrial city of Hengelo walked off the job. Word of their action spread swiftly throughout the country, and soon much of Holland was paralyzed. Miners refused to enter the mines; farmers withheld deliveries of milk and produce. The Germans rounded up strikers by the hundreds and tried them in summary courts, often set up in factories and mills for maximum intimidation. In ten days they sentenced and executed eighty strike leaders. The strike was broken, but the Germans now understood that they would never win over the Dutch people.

Strikes in the industrial regions of France, Belgium, Norway, and Denmark carried the same unmistakable message. In 1943, the entire city of Aalborg in Denmark closed down in protest over an incident tied to the Resistance. Just outside town, German police had surprised a group of Danes obviously waiting for a British airdrop of arms. They shot one of them, a young bank clerk, and on the scheduled day of his funeral, 10,000 people turned up at the cemetery—flouting an order against public assemblies. The police and the mourners clashed, and in the protest that

followed four more people were killed. The whole town went on strike, and within hours the strike had spread across the country, forcing the Germans to put the Danes under martial law. Gone was any hope Berlin might have had that Denmark would be a model German protectorate.

Although the strike as a weapon of resistance never seriously threatened the Germans, it unquestionably strengthened the people's will to resist. Yet the strike could be a double-edged sword. When a labor stoppage went on long enough to hurt the Germans, it was likely to be felt even harder by the civilian population as well, thereby eroding support for the Resistance. The Dutch rail strike of 1944, for example, slowed the movement of supplies to the Germans, but in retaliation the Germans issued an embargo on the import of foodstuffs, which made the bleak "winter of hunger" in Holland much worse for the Dutch. And late in the war the Germans actually exploited the strike by circulating false strike calls, bearing the forged signatures of union leaders—thereby providing themselves with an excuse for ever more ruthless reprisals.

Walkouts and other forms of civil disobedience got much of their impetus from the underground press. Almost from the moment of capitulation, clandestine newspapers, pamphlets, and books began to appear, providing the people with information, exhorting them to organize and resist, and offering practical advice on how to go about it. One of the earliest and most famous of the pamphlets was penned by the French journalist Jean Texcier and appeared in Paris in August 1940, soon after the German victory. Texcier's *Advice to the Occupied* contained thirty-three short, numbered paragraphs of barbed commentary and counsel. Number 8 was "Ever since they have 'occupied' you, they parade in your dishonor. Will you stay to watch? Interest yourself rather in the shopwindow displays. Because at the rate they are filling up their trucks, there will soon be nothing left to buy." Number 30: "You grumble because they oblige you to be home by exactly 11:00 p.m. Innocent. Haven't you understood that this is to let you listen to the English radio?" Texcier later became editor of *Libération*, which first appeared in December 1940 and was one of the best known and most widely circulated underground newspapers.

Many of the underground journals originated in the "snowball letters" of individuals who wrote to friends, asking them to make copies and pass them on. Soon these primitive newsletters were replaced by more sophisticated efforts, written and edited by professionals and distributed by couriers at great personal risk. The journalists did their work in churches, attics, caves, garages, factories, laundries, and in one case in the cavernous cellars of the Sorbonne. An enterprising Dutch publisher even set up his

printing plant in a hollowed-out haystack. The young men and women who delivered the papers concealed them under loads of produce, or at the bottom of shopping bags or suitcases, and passed them out at church entrances, in marketplaces, or at subway exits.

In all, something like 3,500 illegal newspapers were published in western Europe during the occupation. Their readership was greater than that of the heavily censored regular press, their influence so far-reaching that the Germans bent every effort to destroy them. German authorities warned that every editor would be "answerable with his life for further attempts to poison the popular mind," and security agents were everywhere on the prowl.

The growing size and complexity of the underground press made it more vulnerable to exposure and retribution. The weakest part of the operation involved the procurement of newsprint and the distribution of finished papers. The police became adept at spotting the couriers and frequently seized them before they could slip away into the crowds. Under torture, they were liable to implicate others, and the Germans would then follow the chain to its end. When a Paris lawyer was arrested for complicity in the distribution of the tract *Résistance*, the Germans were able to decimate the paper's editorial leadership in a series of eighteen executions and numerous deportations. By diligent police work, the Germans managed also to arrest and execute more than 70 staff members of the Dutch underground paper *Vrij Nederland* and 120 staffers of the newspaper *Trouw*.

What bedeviled the Germans was the ability of underground papers to survive even such blows as these. Both *Vrij Nederland* and *Trouw* continued printing throughout the occupation. The frustrated German Security Service even tried to strike a bargain with the editors of *Trouw:* If the paper agreed to cease publication, the lives of twenty-three *Trouw* writers and editors being held in German jails would be spared. The newspaper refused, and the twenty-three went before a firing squad. The Dutch paper *Het Parool* suffered similar losses in 1942 and 1944, including the arrest of its founder, Frans Goedhart. But it continued to publish without interruption and even to carry editorials bearing Goedhart's pen name. The Germans did not realize they had captured the paper's publisher, thinking him only a member of the *Het Parool* staff, and the staff intended to keep them in the dark. With the help of the Dutch police, who did know Goedhart's true identity, he was able to escape—just a few days before his scheduled execution.

Many publications lasted only a few issues before they were betrayed or

"Let's hope that they still believe in Father Christmas, Heinz," says Goebbels to Himmler in a cartoon appearing in the Dutch underground newspaper *Metro*. The cartoon pokes fun at the Germans' vain attempt to portray Hitler as a beneficent leader.

Dutch Resistance workers turn out underground leaflets on a tabletop printing press. By the end of the war, Holland's illegal presses were producing 350 different clandestine papers, publications that were a powerful stimulus to civil unrest.

otherwise uncovered by the Germans. Among the least fortunate was *Pantagruel*, founded in Paris in October 1940 by Raymond Deiss, one of France's leading music publishers. Deiss was able to publish only sixteen issues before he was arrested and beheaded. Overall, the price paid by the clandestine press was enormous. In Belgium alone about 3,000 editorial people, or 30 percent of those engaged in underground publishing in that country, were executed, and the toll was equally appalling in other countries. Yet for every underground publication closed down, two new ones seemed to appear. In an unintended tribute to their durability, the Germans took to putting out counterfeit copies of some of the leading clandestine newspapers, filling them with misinformation.

But the heavy-handed German forgeries could not compare with the parodies put out by the underground. A classic of its kind was the issue of the *Haarlemse Courant* published by Dutch patriots on June 5, 1944, the day before D-Day. In addition to satires on Goebbels and Hitler, the issue contained a decree by Holland's SS chief, Hanns Rauter, imposing a special curfew on dogs and ducks for their anti-German activities. The Dutch loved it, and the Germans went berserk—in no small measure because they were sure that the Resistance editors had known the date of the Allied Normandy invasion and had timed their parody accordingly. They did not; it was pure happenstance.

For thousands of people in occupied Europe the chief means of resistance was helping those in flight from the Germans. It was the natural

thing to do. One day in the fall of 1940, Etta Shiber, the widow of an American journalist living in Paris, came upon a British officer in hiding at an inn in the French countryside. Impulsively, Mrs. Shiber hid the man in the trunk of her car and drove back to Paris, where some influential friends helped get him out of the country. As Mrs. Shiber warmed to the work, one success led to another. She used bogus credentials to spirit away less seriously injured British and French prisoners from various hospitals. She boldly took ads in the newspapers and in that astonishing fashion found still other soldiers in need of rescue. The woman was caught, of course, and spent long months in prison before the American government could secure her release in exchange for a female German spy.

The security forces were well aware at the outset that many escaped prisoners of war were being sheltered by the population, and the problem grew more complex every year. In prominently displayed proclamations, the Germans warned that anyone caught aiding POWs would be summarily shot. Yet untold numbers of ordinary people, acting on their own like Mrs. Shiber, took in fugitives and helped them escape. One farmer in northern France rescued fifty-seven French and British soldiers by hiding them on the farms of his friends and neighbors. Lucienne Welschinger, a young girl in Strasbourg, hearing of escapees who were trying to make their way south to the Swiss border, undertook on her own initiative to lead them out of town through the fields and direct them on their way. She and the circle of friends who eventually joined her continued their perilous work for two years, until a breach in security by one of the group led to the arrest and execution of Welschinger and four of her comrades.

These early amateur efforts often developed into elaborate and extensive escape circuits, strongly supported by Allied agencies in England. The networks supplied refugees with guides and safe houses, false papers, rations, medicines, compasses, and civilian clothes. The main escape routes from Holland, Belgium, and France went either south toward Switzerland or southwest through unoccupied France to Spain, Portugal, or North Africa. For those fleeing Denmark, the escape was by boat across the Oresund or the Kattegat to Sweden. From Norway, the route ran along Norway's long, sparsely populated coastline to Sweden. And from neutral but helpful Sweden there were numerous ways to get to Britain.

Perhaps 250,000 people moved along these escape routes during the war. The Germans knew they could not track down every network, so they concentrated on destroying the bigger ones. Among the most successful networks was the so-called Comet Line, run by a young Belgian nurse's aide named Andrée de Jongh, who began her clandestine career by sheltering British soldiers after Dunkirk. Using a network of contacts, she often per-

Issues of the illegal newspaper *Frit Danmark* (Free Denmark) flutter from a window in a Copenhagen street *(top)*. The airborne circulars were intended for civilian passers-by who, like the individuals shown at bottom, would pause to gather them before moving on.

sonally led her charges clear across France to the Spanish frontier. In three years, Andrée de Jongh saved 800 Allied fliers before she was trapped in a farmhouse on the Spanish border and sent to Mauthausen concentration camp, where she spent the rest of the war. Another major network was run by a Belgian named Albert-Marie Guérisse, alias Patrick Albert O'Leary. With the help of British intelligence, the "Pat Line" rescued 700 Allied airmen before it was betrayed in 1942 by that rare form of traitor—an escaped British soldier turned Gestapo informer. Guérisse evaded that particular snare, but about fifty of his group were captured and executed. Later he himself was arrested at a rendezvous in Toulouse with a colleague who turned out to be a double agent. Guérisse was sent to Dachau, but survived.

What was certainly the largest and most extraordinary underground network of the war originated in Holland. This was the National Organization for Help to People in Hiding, popularly known as the L.O. Founded by Mrs. Helena Theodora Kuipers-Rietberg, a housewife and mother of five, and Pastor Frits Slomp, a Calvinist minister, the L.O. recruited 15,000 volunteers to shelter and aid 300,000 Dutch citizens who had gone underground to escape arrest or forced labor. The refugees were known as "divers" (onderduikers—"people who go underwater"). The organization found hiding places for the fugitives, and took considerable care to match "hosts" and "guests" for compatible religious views, interests, and vocational and class backgrounds. The documents and ration books provided to the refugees were sometimes forged and sometimes genuine, for a special L.O. division regularly raided government offices to procure documents and destroy lists of names and addresses useful to the Germans.

The Germans and their collaborators made extraordinary efforts to crush underground organizations such as the L.O. Police squads swooped down on churches, theaters, and soccer stadiums for surprise identity checks. Whole villages or sections of cities were cordoned off and searched house by house. New ration books were printed periodically, to be issued only to those reporting in person and presenting an identity card. A reward of forty guldens head money was offered for every Jew denounced, with failure to report being punishable by death. German security agents worked to infiltrate the escape circuits by posing as fugitives. Inevitably, more than 1,000 members of the L.O. were caught and either executed or deported, among them Mrs. Kuipers-Rietberg, who perished at the Ravensbrück concentration camp. By some estimates, one escape-route worker died for every fugitive who got away through the underground. Yet the work of the L.O. went on until the defeat of the occupiers.

One of the great coups of the war was the rescue of what amounted to nearly the entire Jewish population of Denmark in the fall of 1943, and it

Head bowed in concentration, an expert Dutch forger affixes a signature to a false identification card. Such counterfeit documents helped thousands of fugitives, Jews, and Allied soldiers elude capture by the Germans.

was made possible by a remarkable "conspiracy of goodness" that reached
into the ranks of the occupation itself. So long as the Germans maintained
the fiction of Danish "neutrality" and accorded the Danes preferential
treatment, no attempt was made to round up Danish Jews for deportation.
But with the declaration of martial law, the Jews suddenly became liable
for Hitler's "Final Solution." In mid-September 1943, the Führer signed an
order for their secret arrest and deportation. The ax was to descend on the
night of October 1. Three reinforced Security Police companies were to
arrest the first 5,000 or so victims, for whom cargo space had been arranged.
But not everyone in the Nazi camp was confident about the impending
operation. Hitler's own Reich plenipotentiary in Denmark, Werner Best,
feared that the roundup would trigger an open rebellion in the country.
Best expressed his grave doubts to a friend, Georg Duckwitz, shipping

Fleeing persecution in occupied Denmark, a boatload of Jewish refugees approaches Swedish territorial waters. In the fall of 1943, thousands of such Jews embarked for Sweden from ports in Zeeland and Jutland. Fewer than five percent failed to reach Swedish shores.

attaché at the German embassy in Copenhagen. Duckwitz, horrified at the prospect, leaked word of the Nazis' intentions to a high Danish official, and the news quickly spread to the Jewish community.

At the appointed hour, the great raid unfolded—and failed resoundingly. Only a few hundred Jews, most of them too old or sick to be moved, were collected for deportation. The rest had vanished into the homes of non-Jewish friends and neighbors, and into schools, churches, and other institutions. Copenhagen's hospitals "discharged" patients with Jewish names and reregistered them under pseudonyms, or took in healthy Jewish families and gave them false names and charts. Danish fishermen, mobilized by the Resistance, ferried hundreds of boatloads of Jews across the Kattegat to neutral Sweden. Ultimately, almost 7,200 Jews escaped Hitler's orders, and, of those who were deported, not one is known to have

died in the gas chambers. King Christian made such fierce and continuing representations on their behalf that they were sent to the relatively humane Theresienstadt camp and not to an extermination center.

As the war wore on, Resistance fighters waged an unceasing campaign of espionage, sabotage, and deadly force. The Wehrmacht had scarcely marched into Paris on June 14, 1940, when German soldiers started paying for their victory with their lives—shot as they strolled the streets, stabbed in back alleys, garroted in movie theaters and bawdy houses. The bloodying of the oppressors occurred throughout the occupied lands, but it did not accelerate to major proportions until 1943, when German setbacks in Africa and Russia encouraged many people to believe that Hitler might actually lose the war. By then, too, the Nazis' savage campaign against the Jews and the mounting toll of German terror turned many passive resisters into active ones. In addition, intensified German efforts to recruit forced labor for German farms and factories forced thousands to choose between fight or flight. And finally, the British secret services, later joined by their American counterparts, increasingly furnished both the means and the training that armed resistance required.

The Allied organization most intimately concerned with active resistance groups was the British Special Operations Executive, or SOE. Established by Prime Minister Winston Churchill in the summer of 1940 to "coordinate all actions by way of subversion and sabotage against the enemy overseas," the SOE sent 7,000 agents and instructors to the Continent, some of them by air, some overland through Spain or Portugal, others by sea. Included were telegraphers, saboteurs, spies, propagandists, and liaison officers. Perhaps their most important initial task was to coordinate and sift the immense volume of intelligence available in western Europe and transmit it to London. As one Resistance leader remarked, almost every Frenchman was a potential Allied spy, and the same could be said of people in the other occupied countries. When textile factories in Belgium, for example, started to manufacture tropical uniforms in January 1941, word got out at once and was passed to the British, who surmised that the Germans were planning operations in North Africa. Powerless to prevent leaks of this sort, the Germans concentrated on the networks that collected and forwarded raw intelligence.

Particularly at risk were the SOE radio operators who constituted the critical link between occupied Europe and England. The first dozen operators who parachuted into France in 1941 and made their way to a safe house in Marseilles found the Gestapo waiting for them, directed there by an address book retrieved from a captured agent's pocket. With experience,

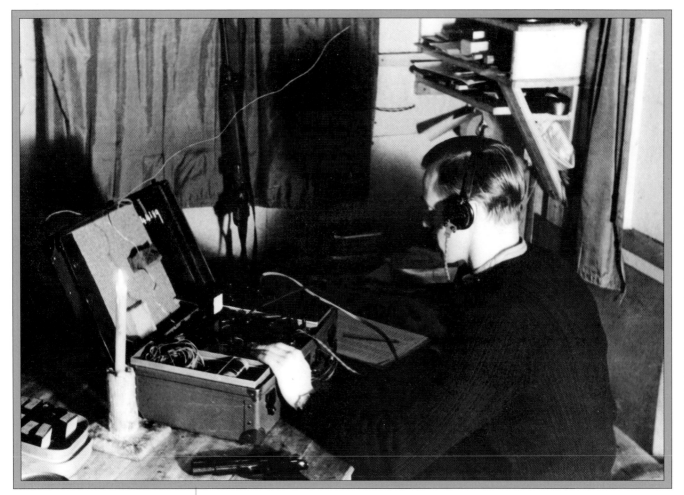

By candlelight, with a pistol and carbine close at hand, a Norwegian radio agent uses a portable "suitcase" transceiver to tap out a coded message for Special Operations Executive (SOE) headquarters in London.

the SOE became more adept at slipping its agents into the occupied countries, but their existence was always precarious, with an average survival time of less than six months. Radio operators were particularly vulnerable to detection by special Gestapo-Abwehr tracking teams. Operating in vehicles disguised as ambulances or delivery vans that were equipped with sophisticated direction finders, these mobile units could quickly pinpoint an operator's position, particularly if he transmitted several times in succession from the same location. Special Operations Executive operators were advised to move around constantly and were instructed, if caught, to swallow the cyanide tablet that was part of their gear rather than risk disclosing under torture their codes and schedules.

Most often, German counterintelligence was less interested in closing down SOE circuits than in "turning" them to their own use. In the event an SOE operator was taken alive, he was supposed to insert a prearranged "mistake" into the first group of letters in his next transmission; this would alert London that he was transmitting under duress. But if this failed, as it sometimes did, and the Gestapo-Abwehr teams got control of the SOE man and his transmitter, they would imitate the telegrapher's "fist," or touch on the key, and start relaying false information. The ultimate aim of the *Funkspiel*, or radio game, was to create phantom Resistance networks to which the Allies would drop additional agents and large quantities of supplies, along with documents of vital importance to the German Security Police. Once they captured a network, the Germans went to extraordinary lengths to give it legitimacy, even to the point of smuggling an occasional

The Odyssey of a Patriot Pair

On August 11, 1944, Olaf Ellefsen sat huddled over a radio transmitter in his tiny farmhouse on Norway's north coast. An agent of the British Secret Intelligence Service (SIS), which tracked German naval movements around Norway, Ellefsen was trying to contact headquarters with a crucial piece of information—the position of a German steamer carrying fifty captured Norwegian Resistance fighters. British warships in the Norwegian Sea were poised to intercept the vessel and reclaim the prisoners.

The message never got sent. Just as Ellefsen established contact with Home Station outside London, his wife, Aslaug, who had been keeping watch at the window, interrupted him with a warning: "Olaf! Germans! The radio car!" Advancing along the road was a radio surveil-lance truck, its antenna trained menacingly on the couple's house.

The Ellefsens, recent SIS recruits who were expecting the birth of their first child in a month, had been caught red-handed. Some forty Gestapo agents converged on the house, and finding the hastily concealed transmitter under a bedspread, savagely beat Olaf with their weapons. Ordered to reestablish radio contact with Home Station, a bloodied but resolute Olaf secretly transmitted, "Germans taken me." The rescue mission was scrubbed.

Fearful that he would talk under torture, Olaf seized his one opportunity for escape: During a visit to the outhouse, he clobbered his guard and broke for the woods. An intensive search failed to turn him up, and a week later the resourceful agent crossed into neutral Sweden.

Aslaug was taken to a detention camp in Tromso, then to Oslo where, under heavy Gestapo guard, she gave birth to a son on September 9. Named for his father, little Olaf remained with his mother in a hospital through Christmas. With the New Year, however, came the news that baby Olaf would be placed with his grandmother; Aslaug—Norway's only female SIS agent—would enter Grini concentration camp, outside Oslo, alone.

A Gestapo officer arrived to take the child on the appointed day. Moments before leaving, he was detained by a phone call, talked briefly, and then turned to the grieving Aslaug: The case against her had been dismissed, he said without further explanation. Aslaug and the child were set free, and in May 1945 they were reunited with Olaf.

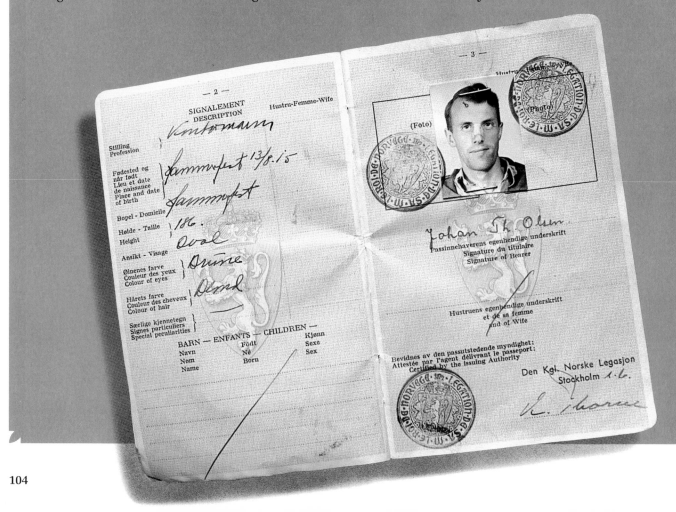

A coded message *(above)* sent to Olaf Ellefsen in Sweden informs him of efforts to free his wife, Aslaug, who was being held under German guard in Oslo. The deciphered text reads, "Stockholm is in the process of trying to get Aslaug out and across to Sweden. Best regards, Teodor. Ends." The communiqué's sender was Eric "Teodor" Welsh, director of the Norway section of Britain's Secret Intelligence Service.

◁ Shortly after escaping from his German captors, Ellefsen obtained this false passport *(opposite)* in the name Johan Th. Olsen from the Norwegian legation in Stockholm. The gash on his forehead and his bandaged nose attest to the brutal treatment he suffered at the hands of the Gestapo.

A beaming Aslaug Ellefsen dandles baby Olaf in this photograph taken shortly after their surprise release from the custody of the German secret police in early 1945. The reason for their sudden liberation remains unknown.

downed Allied flier back into England. At one time, German agents were running eleven French Resistance transmitters simultaneously—with the result that in 1943 more than half of all airdrops over France fell into their hands. So adroit was the deception that it was not until the Normandy invasion that British intelligence learned that certain Resistance groups on which they had counted did not exist.

All told, one-third of all SOE radio operators sent into Europe were taken by the Germans. Yet the number of clandestine radio networks grew steadily, until by the time of invasion, close to 100 operators were sending out 6,000 reports a day from France alone. The Belgian prime-minister-in-exile remarked that the underground radio had turned his country into a glass house for the Allied supreme command.

No radio operator was ever hunted with more determination—or less success—than a young Norwegian named Einar Skinnarland, who played a key role in one of the war's great triumphs of sabotage. In early 1942, Skinnarland installed himself on the rugged Hardanger Plateau of south-central Norway, near the Norsk Hydro installation, which was producing significant quantities of heavy water for use in German nuclear research. From his concealed position, Skinnarland maintained radio communication with London for nearly a year, sending information about the Norsk plant and its defenses. After lengthy and elaborate planning, a team of six Norwegians parachuted in from Britain on the night of February 17, 1943, joining three others who had already arrived. The men scaled an ice-sheathed cliff to the power plant, swiftly overcame the guards, and blew up eighteen of the heavy-water-producing cells. The enraged Germans deployed 3,000 troops to comb the area, but every one of the saboteurs, including the canny Skinnarland, made his escape.

Norsk Hydro was out of commission for five months, and when it started up again the plant was then partially destroyed by a massive American bombing raid. Finally, in February 1944, Norwegian saboteurs ended the Reich's nuclear ambitions for good by sinking a train ferry carrying the remaining stock of heavy water as it crossed from Norway to Germany.

Industrial sabotage on a modest scale had disrupted German plans from the start of the occupation. At first such activity simply involved deliberate slowdown tactics and blunders on the production lines. After the occupation, Luxembourg's normally efficient steel mills inexplicably dropped to one-third of their previous production. A Danish shipyard somehow took twenty-six months instead of the usual nine to deliver a minesweeper for the German navy, while the managers of a Belgian arms factory expressed deep embarrassment over delivering 1,500,000 cartridges without gunpowder. French railroad workers absent-mindedly threw the wrong

switches, thereby managing to "lose" whole trains; sand and emery dust found their way into axle boxes; a little acid or a few baskets of rotten vegetables were dumped into carloads of produce en route to Germany.

Unable to pinpoint those responsible, the Germans countered with random arrests. But these had so little effect that sabotage in Denmark increased tenfold between 1940 and 1943. The Danes, who enjoyed keeping score, totted up 119 train derailments, 1,525 rail lines cut, 58 locomotives blown up, along with 31 railroad bridges. Also sabotaged to some degree were 2,700 industrial sites in Denmark, plus various German military repair shops, vehicles, aircraft, and naval vessels, for which no tally was available. So severe was the sabotage that Field Marshal Gerd von Rundstedt, commander in chief of the German forces in the west, was moved to speak of a "serious turning point" in the German logistics effort in 1943.

Heinrich Himmler, whose SS was now responsible for maintaining order in the occupied lands, mobilized fresh forces to fight the Resistance. In every country Himmler's deputies organized and armed scores of special "auxiliary services" to wage war against the Resistance. The Dutch, for example, had to contend with the paramilitary Schalkhaar police, recipients of special SS training, and the so-called V-men, undercover agents charged with infiltrating underground organizations. In France, 45,000 Frenchmen flocked to join the infamous Milice, a nationwide French equivalent of the German Gestapo set up in 1943 at the suggestion of Hitler. For a time, in fact, there were probably as many Frenchmen enlisted in the German-run security forces as there were in the Resistance.

These special auxiliaries existed side by side with the traditional forces of law and order, but they were very different in character. The special auxiliaries often proved more zealous than the Germans themselves. "The dogs were worse than the master," remarked a Danish Resistance fighter bitterly. The traditional police did not take kindly to the pro-Nazi newcomers and increasingly balked at assignments that brought them up against the Resistance. This was particularly true in small towns, where the police warned their neighbors of impending danger and refused to arrest Jews for deportation. Indeed, in Holland, entire police units went underground, and those that remained were so undependable that in 1944 the Germans took away their arms. Meanwhile, the refusal of the Danish police to combat the Resistance or protect factories from sabotage so incensed the SS chief Günther Pancke that he ordered the entire 10,000-man national police force arrested and sent to Buchenwald. About 1,700 men were rounded up, but the rest eluded capture.

By 1943, Resistance groups were escalating attacks on individual Germans and prominent collaborators. The underground tried its victims *in*

absentia and turned over their names to assassination squads. Sometimes collaborators were forewarned of their fate with a little coffin in the mail. A hit team in Holland gunned down a former minister of war and a one-time chief of the general staff, both notorious Nazi sympathizers. Dutch assassins also did away with the undersecretary for propaganda and the Nazi mayors of several towns. Overall, more than forty civilian Nazi sympathizers were slain in the first six months of 1943 in Holland. And there was no compunction about the killings. "The assassination of a collaborator is a liquidation, not a murder," advised an underground newspaper. Meanwhile, in France, where the Resistance had a saying, *"à chacun son Boche"*—"to each man his German"—there were no fewer than 281 assassination attempts on Germans, 97 on French police, and 147 on French collaborators during the same period.

The German response was savage. From the very first, German policy had been to execute 50, even 100 hostages for every German slain by the Resistance. And sabotage, indeed any overt act of resistance, was dealt with only a little less harshly. As early as September 1941, Hitler had issued his infamous *Nacht und Nebel,* or night and fog, decree. People suspected of anti-Reich activities would simply vanish into the night and fog; families, friends, national authorities would never hear of them again, never know where they had been sent, or whether they were alive or dead. Something

German soldiers survey the wreckage of Copenhagen's General Motors factory, demolished by the Danish Resistance in February 1944. The plant was sabotaged to prevent the Germans from using the cars and spare parts manufactured there to aid its war effort.

like 7,000 people were consigned to this eerie oblivion in the course of the war. One of the few survivors, a Norwegian Resistance member named Arne Brun Lie, arrested when he was sixteen, later testified to a year of beatings and tortures at various concentration camps. He remembered how a Gestapo guard once shrieked at him: "You are already dead. You are mysterious, marvelous living dead. You are anonymous. *Nacht und Nebel*. Next to your number there is no name. Only the living have names. We crush you, swat you, exterminate you into *Nacht und Nebel*, the night of the noose, the fog of the crematorium."

As the Germans realized that the war was turning in the Allies' favor, they began to rely more heavily on additional terrorizing decrees issued from Hitler's headquarters: the Bullet Decree, which directed that all saboteurs be executed on the spot, and the Family Hostage Law, which gave the security forces the authority to shoot all male relatives of fleeing terrorists and condemn female relatives to hard labor and children to reform school.

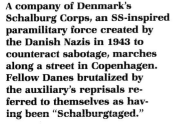

A company of Denmark's Schalburg Corps, an SS-inspired paramilitary force created by the Danish Nazis in 1943 to counteract sabotage, marches along a street in Copenhagen. Fellow Danes brutalized by the auxiliary's reprisals referred to themselves as having been "Schalburgtaged."

With greater frequency, the Germans chose victims from the group of offenders called *Todeskandidaten*, or death candidates. They were either Resistance suspects or simply political prisoners and prominent citizens designated for execution as reprisal in the event of terrorist acts.

The bloodbath grew ever greater as the Germans turned their fury on entire towns. When two Gestapo officers were killed during an attack on a Resistance camp in Televag, Norway, the village was razed, its fishing fleet sunk, its cattle slaughtered, its male inhabitants sent to death camps, and its women and children to internment camps. In Amsterdam, crowds were forced to witness the burning of homes and the execution of twenty-nine hostages in retaliation for the assassination of a Ger-

Dutch Resistance agents stash firearms and ammunition under the floorboards of an Amsterdam bathroom for later use against the German occupiers. The penalty for such activity could be summary execution by the Germans.

man double agent. "The bodies remained in the road under the smoke of the burning houses," one witness recalled. In an orgy of murder, 263 Dutch lost their lives when a group of Resistance fighters set out to hijack a Wehrmacht truck carrying 6,000 pounds of pork. Hearing what sounded like a truck approaching, the men stepped out in the road to halt it. The vehicle turned out to be a German staff car, a powerful BMW, carrying General Hanns Rauter, SS commander of the Netherlands. In the ensuing gunfight, Rauter was badly wounded, and the Germans saw the ambush as an attempt on his life. In swift and terrible retribution, they lined up the prisoners in a number of Dutch jails and shot them all. More than 100 of the massacred men were left lying along the road at the site of the ambush, with a notice that said, "This is what we do to terrorists and saboteurs."

Often random attacks on individuals and institutions were carried out

by plain-clothes squads to confuse the public about who was responsible. In Denmark, German terror teams made up a card file of victims to be shot and buildings to be blown up. In their first foray, the anonymous killers forced their way into the home of a leading parliamentarian and patriot and shot him dead. Other attacks quickly followed, on Danish doctors, lawyers, journalists, academics, and artists. After a well-known Danish clergyman and playwright named Kaj Munk condemned such behavior from the pulpit and affirmed the right to resist, he was dragged from his home by several unidentified men and shot in the street. In a sixteen-month period the murder squads killed 899 Danish civilians.

German bomb squads were every bit as busy in Denmark. Time bombs exploded in movie theaters and hotel lobbies. The Copenhagen students'

Gunned down by machine-gun fire early on the morning of September 13, 1944, two Danes, pro-German radio propagandists and suspected informers, lie dead on a quiet residential street in a suburb of Copenhagen. A special Resistance "liquidation committee" carried out the assassinations.

hostel and the Royal Copenhagen porcelain factory were blown up, along with the editorial offices of sixteen provincial newspapers. Then, in the ultimate retaliatory blow, a squad from the Schalburg Corps, a Danish Nazi paramilitary force, entered Copenhagen's beloved Tivoli Gardens in the dead of night with bags of explosives and totally destroyed the entire complex—the concert hall, the sports arena, the amusement park, the dance pavilion, even the magical "Glass House." The destruction was intended to punish the Danes for daring to celebrate en masse the Allied landing on the Normandy beaches.

The French also suffered grievously. To avenge the shooting of a German officer, German troops massacred 639 people in the village of Oradour-sur-Glane. Despite such draconian measures, a general order to the German army in 1944 asserted that "the action taken is never sufficiently severe." And so the Germans sought ways to make the executions more visible, more terrifying. In the city of Tulle, in reprisal for partisan activities ninety-nine men, women, and boys were seized and hanged from balconies, window grilles, and lampposts along the main street, while their families and friends were forced to watch. Although no one knows the exact toll, perhaps 30,000 hostages were executed in France alone.

The mass terror undoubtedly had some effect on the Resistance. Dutch leaders, for example, thought better of a plan to assassinate the notorious Anton Mussert, Holland's chief Nazi, because of the hideous reprisals that were certain to follow. Yet even the worst brutality against civilians could not stamp out the Resistance, and while the terror continued to the end, the Germans increasingly found that they were able to achieve greater success with another weapon: the largely silent and unseen counterespionage forces of the Gestapo and its offshoots.

The Gestapo, aided by agents drawn from the ranks of the infamous Milice, the French fascist police, enjoyed a number of successes against the Resistance in France. German strategy was based on the assumption that the Resistance circuits in France were all linked, and that by penetrating one network, others could be exposed. In this they were quite right, for the Allies had played into their hands.

The British, particularly the SOE agents in the field, strongly favored independent circuits, sealed off from one another to reduce the consequences of betrayal. But General Charles de Gaulle, leader of the Free French, demanded a resistance organization of interdependent circuits operating from a central command under strong Free French influence. In the end, de Gaulle prevailed—and the Germans had the satisfaction of capturing the man designated by de Gaulle to command all French resistance. He was Jean Moulin, former prefect of the department of Eure-

Using piles of spent cartridges as clues, German military investigators *(right)* assume the positions of Dutch Resistance fighters who ambushed a BMW carrying Nazi leader Hanns Rauter, his orderly, and his driver on the night of March 6, 1945. The assault, believed by the Germans to be a deliberate attempt on Rauter's life, was in fact a random effort by the Resistance to commandeer a vehicle. When the Germans resisted, the orderly and the driver—shown above, slumped over the wheel—died in a hail of submachine-gun fire. Rauter, the most powerful SS official in occupied Holland, survived multiple wounds, including one to the jaw *(above left)*. The attackers were never caught, but the Germans avenged the deed by executing 263 Dutch people throughout Holland.

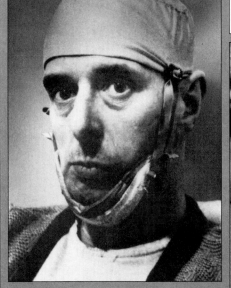

et-Loir, who had opposed the Germans from the start and, naturally, had been arrested for this effrontery. Upon his eventual release, he had escaped to London, where he impressed de Gaulle, who had him parachuted back into France with the mission of uniting the many major Resistance groups. Moulin had succeeded brilliantly at this formidable task, setting up a National Resistance Council subject to direction from London. But then he fell victim to the system's inherent weakness.

In the spring of 1943 at a routine street blockade in Marseilles, the Gestapo arrested one Jean Multon, a chief of the Resistance circuit known as Mouvements unis de la Résistance, or MUR. Multon, not a strong man, bargained for his life. Through him, the Germans and their agents seized the Marseilles headquarters of the MUR and arrested 125 Resistance fighters in the Marseilles area. That was only a beginning. Multon's contacts in the Resistance extended far beyond his individual network. Within two months, the Gestapo had captured dozens of other Resistance members, including Jean Moulin who was arrested in a doctor's office in Caluire-et-Cuire, a suburb of Lyons, as he was holding a meeting of Resistance leaders, urgently called to deal with the unraveling of their circuits. The unfortunate Moulin died under torture rather than reveal what he knew, but others at the meeting revealed enough for the Germans to destroy several circuits, capturing and executing key agents.

Yet Moulin's death was not a total loss. One of his major goals had been the formation of an underground army, ready to rise against the Germans at the time of invasion. The result was the Forces françaises de l'intérieur (FFI), a paramilitary organization of 30,000 men trained and equipped by the Allies. Augmenting the FFI were tens of thousands of "maquis," young men who had gone into the mountains, forests, and scrublands to avoid forced labor in Germany. Many of the maquis were already practiced in sabotage and assassination. Now the Allies sought to incorporate them into the main Resistance movement. They provided weapons, explosives, and instruction in demolition and guerrilla tactics, and dispatched liaison teams to coordinate their efforts. Nevertheless, the maquis remained largely unstructured and often poorly armed. A maquis band of 150 men in the Creuse district of south-central France could muster only 35 revolvers, 13 rifles, 3 submachine guns, and 6 grenades. The scanty arsenal was a tribute to German skill at intercepting Allied airdrops.

Before the Allied invasion, both the FFI and the maquis were under orders to restrict themselves to sabotage and occasional raids on German supply lines. To counter this hit-and-run campaign, the Germans sought to lure the resistants into the sort of open battle they were ill-equipped to fight. The strategy often worked. At Glières in the Haute-Savoie, a hot-

headed former lieutenant in the Chasseurs alpins (Alpine Infantry) led 500 FFI against a force of German infantry and lost half his men. At Beyssenac, near Limoges, a maquis band challenged an SS unit; the maquis leader bleakly reported that his men had been wiped out "without even wounding a single SS man." After the Normandy invasion larger actions, involving thousands of maquis and FFI members, were launched against the Germans in anticipation of speedy assistance from Allied forces. But the attacks were poorly conceived and coordinated, and the Allies, in any case, had their hands full breaking out of Normandy. The Resistance forces were, more often than not, defeated.

The most calamitous defeat occurred shortly after the invasion on the rugged Alpine plateau of Vercors, near Grenoble, in the southeast corner of France. There a combined FFI and maquis force of 3,500 men unfurled the French flag and declared the Free Republic of Vercors while awaiting reinforcements they thought the Allies were planning to send in by air. Instead, two German divisions—more than 10,000 heavily armed men—converged on the 300-square-mile natural fortress in a two-pronged assault from north and south, pushing the defenders back into an area of cliffs and caves. Then, at a crucial moment, twenty glider-towing aircraft swooped out of the sky. The overjoyed French thought that the Allies had arrived.

Under the Nazi flag, a German tribunal in occupied Paris *(above)* hears testimony in the "trial" of twenty-seven reputed members of the militant Communist Youth Battalion, charged with assassination and sabotage. At top right, German guards lead handcuffed defendants from the courtroom following the April 1942 judgment in which twenty-five received death sentences. Of these, two were granted stays-of-execution: Simone Schloss, shown outside the judicial chambers *(right)*, and Marie-Thérèse Lefèvre, both of whom were sent to Anrath prison in Germany. Some months later, Schloss was decapitated.

But it was the Germans—200 elite Waffen-SS troops, who landed in the meadows behind the Resistance forces and assailed them from the rear. The French fought valiantly, and the battle dragged on for two days. But in the end the Resistance fighters were crushed, with more than 1,000 dead.

When Allied troops finally began to drive across France, they called on the Resistance to help them in three ways: by stepping up industrial sabotage, by destroying Germany's overland supply lines, and by harassing German troop movements. Saboteurs blew up 800 locomotives and devastated what remained of the French rail system. A senior German intelligence officer in southern France recorded that rail traffic in his district "was completely paralyzed by sabotage." Yet this same officer noted that the roads remained relatively free for motor convoys, which meant that "supply columns and disengaging movements were unpleasantly but not significantly disrupted." The truth of the matter was that while the FFI eventually managed to mobilize nearly 400,000 men, they were too lightly armed and too poorly trained to do more than harass the Germans. French armed resistance was not in itself formidable enough to cause a major shift in German strategy or a redistribution of German troops.

The same was largely true elsewhere in western Europe. The home armies mobilized in Holland, Denmark, and Norway were brilliant in sabotage but were never strong enough to stand up to regular German forces, and for the most part wisely did not try. Only the Belgian underground army played an active role in the nation's liberation, assisting the British in capturing Antwerp's invaluable port facilities intact. But the Belgians did not go into action until after the British 11th Armored Division approached the dock area. All the home armies, in fact, were held in check by the Allied command for fear that they would obstruct the overall strategy. Indeed, the Resistance-led uprising in Paris in August 1944 forced the Allies to abandon their plans to bypass the city and tied up troops and supplies that could have been used in the advance.

All in all, concluded one high-ranking German officer, the Resistance forces "played no decisive part in the fighting." In a purely military sense his assessment was true; fewer than 20 of the 300 German divisions deployed in Europe in 1944 were committed to internal security, and they were mostly second-line troops. But the psychological effect on the Germans was enormous. The sabotage and civil disobedience, the assassinations, the spying, the vast escape apparatus, the hostility visible on virtually every face, and the mounting German frustration in dealing with it all, shook the occupiers' faith in themselves. And that faith—in the correctness of their cause, in their superiority over other peoples, in their inherent right to rule—had been crucial to the Germans' success thus far. ✚

Horrified residents of Autun in east-central France survey the carnage wrought by the German execution of some twenty-five members of the Régiment de Valmy, Resistance fighters who staged an abortive attempt to free the town from Nazi occupation in September 1944.

The Cold Shoulder from Denmark

Less than twenty-four hours after Germany's lightning conquest of Denmark on April 9, 1940, a beleaguered King Christian X instructed his people: "The German troops now in the country are acting in association with the Danish defense power, and it is the duty of the population to abstain from any resistance to those troops." So earnestly did the Danes adhere to their sovereign's plea for conciliation that Hitler dubbed the tiny nation his "pet canary." As time would tell, it was a wholly inappropriate epithet.

What Hitler mistook for weakness was, in fact, pragmatism. Realizing that its army of 14,500 troops was no match for Germany's military colossus, Denmark settled for an uneasy truce: As long as Germany's occupation forces—ostensibly there to safeguard Denmark against attack—did not threaten the Danes' constitutional rights, Denmark would endure the invaders peaceably. Germany rewarded its "model protectorate" by permitting the king and his government to remain in power; a single diplomat—the German ambassador—represented the Reich's official interests.

In time, however, this forced union began to show signs of strain. Subtly, with a thousand subversive gestures, the Danes sought to undermine their "protectors": The friendly overtures of German soldiers met with the Danish *kolde Skulder* (cold shoulder), and saboteurs began to harass the occupiers. In the March 1943 general elections, the Danish Nazi party drew a paltry two percent of the vote.

By the summer of 1943, the Danes' contempt for the Germans had grown blatant; mass demonstrations choked city streets, and acts of sabotage more than doubled—from 93 in July to 220 in August. The Germans retaliated by imposing curfews and interning Danes in labor camps. These measures only fueled Danish restiveness. Finally, on August 24, in the boldest act of insurrection yet, Resistance agents dynamited the Forum Exhibition Hall near Copenhagen just hours before its formal rededication as a German army barracks. The blast—heard for miles around—signaled an ominous change in Danish-German relations.

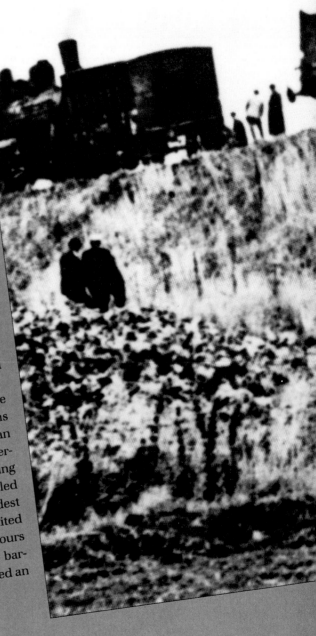

Danish civilians examine the wreckage of a train derailed in Jutland by the Danish Resistance on August 23, 1943, in the underground war against the German occupiers.

Danish police struggle to quell an uprising in Odense on August 24, 1943, in which the townspeople, angered at continued government compliance with the occupation forces, overturned a police van.

A German sharpshooter in a horse-drawn wagon stands ready to fire during a patrol of Odense's riot-torn streets. The same marksman later shot a local woman in the neck.

A Season of Insurgency

Well before the Forum explosion, the commander of the German occupation forces, General Hermann von Hanneken, had informed Berlin of the escalating insurgency in the country. In July, saboteurs at the Odense Steel Shipyard had severely damaged a new minesweeper; outraged German authorities countered by posting armed guards to keep watch on the shipyard workers, who promptly called a strike. A wave of sympathy strikes paralyzed local businesses. The Germans responded with military patrols and twilight curfews.

Appeals by the government for a return to "calm and order" only intensified worker agitation. Early August brought another sabotage attempt at the Odense shipyard, followed by German reprisals. The workers answered with a citywide general strike on August 18, which quickly spread to Esbjerg, Aalborg, and Skagen. Within a fortnight, industries in seventeen Danish cities had ground to a halt. Finally, when rioting workers in Odense nearly bludgeoned a German officer to death, Berlin took radical steps to regain control.

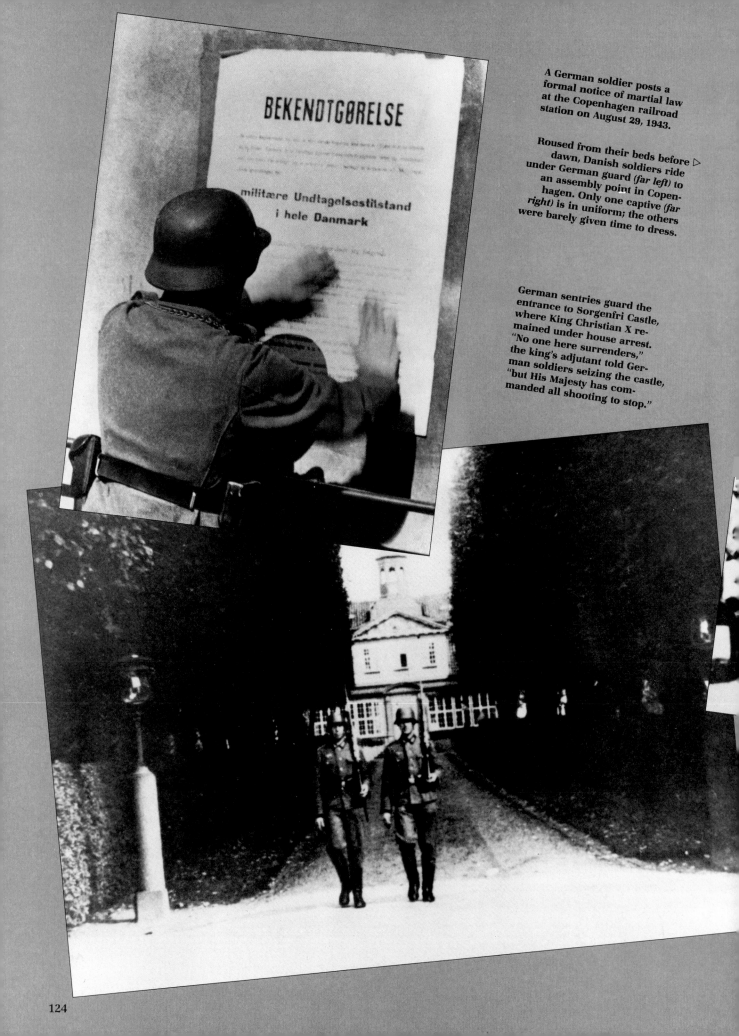

BEKENDTGØRELSE

**militære Undtagelsestilstand
i hele Danmark**

A German soldier posts a formal notice of martial law at the Copenhagen railroad station on August 29, 1943.

Roused from their beds before ▷ dawn, Danish soldiers ride under German guard (*far left*) to an assembly point in Copenhagen. Only one captive (*far right*) is in uniform; the others were barely given time to dress.

German sentries guard the entrance to Sorgenfri Castle, where King Christian X remained under house arrest. "No one here surrenders," the king's adjutant told German soldiers seizing the castle, "but His Majesty has commanded all shooting to stop."

In the Grip of Martial Law

On August 28, 1943, the German ambassador delivered an ultimatum to the Danish prime minister: Resistance must stop, or the Germans would impose martial law. The Danes must cease all strikes and public gatherings, adhere to stringent curfews, capture those guilty of beating the German officer in Odense, and enforce the death penalty for sabotage. They would have seven hours to respond.

Fifteen minutes before the deadline, the Danes answered with an unequivocal no. Berlin's reaction was immediate. German soldiers seized every power station, railroad yard, and industrial facility in Denmark. The nation's natural leaders—politicians, professors, businessmen, and soldiers—were taken to detention camps. After a scuffle with the Danish Royal Guard, German troops took over Sorgenfri Castle and placed the king under house arrest. With a ring of panzers surrounding Copenhagen, the Wehrmacht was in total control.

In a display of German military might, a panzer carrying a contingent of soldiers stands menacingly on a street in Copenhagen.

A German motorized detachme (top) takes possession of the prison camp at Horserød, whe citizens arrested in the preda sweep of Denmark's cities are be interned. Below, the camp Danish administrators and guards are shown exiting the facility on August 29, 1943.

Caught in a German Net

To house the hundreds of Danish citizens taken prisoner during the Wehrmacht's crackdown on August 29, the Germans seized a prison camp in Horserød, twenty-five miles northwest of Copenhagen, and replaced the Danish guards with Nazi soldiers. The camp had been established originally by the Danes on German orders in June 1941 to confine Danish Communists. Now the prison was expanded to include some of Denmark's most influential citizens. Ironically, the Germans were forced to release several bureaucrats among the new prisoners within hours of their incarceration so that they could restart the stalled machinery of Danish government—by then officially under German control.

Nazi soldiers gather at a corner of Horserød camp, from which a hundred of the Communist inmates managed to escape during the German takeover.

Despite orders to "surrender under protest," Danish soldiers in Holbæk prepare to fight.

Bemused German soldiers survey a pile of broken weapons surrendered by the Danish army in response to demands to disarm.

Cracking Down on the Danes

At the same time the Germans were arresting Danish citizens and occupying government offices and industrial facilities, they were also storming Danish army installations. Recognizing the futility of armed resistance, the commander in chief of the Danish army, General Ebbe Goertz, ordered a cease-fire. By noon on August 29, Denmark's army was under German control.

The Danish navy fared better. When the Germans attacked the main naval base at Copenhagen at 4:00 a.m. on the 29th, Danish sailors—operating under standing orders—systematically detonated charges planted in the hulls of some ships or fled in others. Within the space of an hour, twenty-nine Danish warships had been sunk. Thirteen escaped to safe harbor in Sweden. The few remaining vessels—all small naval craft—became spoils for the Reich.

Listing after two explosions in
its hull, the Danish gunboat
Peder Skram takes on water
at the Copenhagen naval base,
where the command has gone
out to "escape or scuttle."

Living through the Limbo Years

Children at a nursery in occupied Paris sit down to a lunch of watery soup. Communal soup kitchens were common during the occupation, as were "rescos," or restaurants that served cheap meals to low-income families.

hortly before noon one summer day in 1940, citizens of a small village south of the Gironde estuary in southwestern France were stunned to see a German motorcyclist roar into town. He carried a pink slip to be delivered to the mayor: Sixty rooms would be required for German soldiers that very night. "It had been rumored that the enemy were north of the Gironde," a villager wrote to a friend a few days later, "but no one dreamed that they could be so close to us. The constable hurriedly posted notices on the church, the hotel, and the corner house, inviting the population to be calm and dignified and to go about their ordinary pursuits. For once, the women did not have much to say. In groups of three and four, they stood in the middle of the street, whispering."

By four o'clock, the streets were filled with the smooth hum of well-tuned German engines. "A stream of swift vehicles, lead-colored, solid-tired, was purring and rumbling towards Le Verdun," the Frenchman wrote. "Slender-nosed artillery, trailed by trucks of ammunition; motorcycles with sidecars, plastered with spare wheels; three-seated open cars, four soldiers to a seat, each with a short rifle between his knees. Their machinery was magnificent. From behind a plane tree I viewed the procession until darkness shut it out, without hearing a bolt rattle or a spark plug fail."

When the column finally passed, it left behind a contingent of soldiers and officers billeted in the town. Several were lodged in the writer's own guest room. Their behavior was irreproachable, scrupulously correct, unfailingly polite. The officers curbed any tendency toward rowdiness in their troops, keeping the rawboned young soldiers on such a tight rein that on the first day only three were permitted to enter the local café at a time.

Soon the stiff, mutually wary relations between newcomers and townsfolk began to ease. On the third day, one soldier broke the ice by stooping down to play with a puppy; another waved at a little girl. "After the lapse of a week, though still reserved and keeping to themselves, they had become integrated with the landscape. The village had ceased to accord them much attention," wrote the Frenchman. He added that the invaders seemed intent on "accomplishing their task with a minimum of friction."

Precisely what that task was, or how long it would take, remained to be seen. The letter continued:

"As to the future, our village is holding its breath with its fingers crossed. Now and again there is a stray straw in the wind. The boys who occupy our pink guest room find the color effeminate. They say that if I will buy the paint and wallpaper, they themselves will do the manual work of redecoration, in the best Munich manner. 'But do you think it will be worth the trouble for so short a time?' I question."

"Oh yes," came the reply that made the letter writer's heart sink into his shoes. "They say we are to be with you for five years."

The letter, smuggled to an American writer named Elizabeth Morrow, was one of a series relating how the German invasion and the early months of occupation affected one ordinary middle-class French family. But virtually the same story could have been told in almost any western European town where the inhabitants watched the invaders roll in, their bristling weaponry and "magnificent" machinery making them seem as inevitable and unstoppable as some great force of nature. And indeed, the resultant changes, while not so physically dramatic as those wrought by flood, earthquake, or tornado, were in some ways equally severe.

As the dust of blitzkrieg settled and the initial fear, confusion, and disorder gave way to weary resignation, the people of western Europe tried to pick up their lives and get on with things. But they found that all the familiar, prosaic routines of everyday life had been altered. Going to work, buying groceries, doing business at the bank, reading a newspaper, writing a letter, taking a bus: All became difficult, complicated, even dangerous.

It was true that Denmark, Norway, France, and the Low Countries were not fated to suffer the nightmare of naked brutality that had so recently engulfed Poland—at least not immediately. Instead, the peoples of occupied western Europe seemed to experience a kind of bad dream. In this nightmare, the well-educated and prosperous inhabitants of one of the wealthiest, most productive regions of the globe would witness their homelands transformed by oppression and privation into unfamiliar, backward, and increasingly dangerous territory, as if the entire continent had fallen under an evil spell.

"In these months of desolate isolation, occupied France has indeed become unrecognizable, has slipped off and back through time and space until it has missed its hold on the 1941 calendar and seems without date," wrote Janet Flanner, Paris correspondent for the *New Yorker* magazine, less than a year after the fall of France. "It has lost its proper physical place on the map of Europe and could be somewhere out in limbo, an island

Danish villagers mingle easily with German troops early in the occupation. The lack of Danish resistance to the invasion helped ease tensions between the Danes and their occupiers during the first part of the war.

surrounded by land, where travellers cannot explore or the inhabitants write letters, where the telegraph ceases to operate as if it had never been invented; where food has again become a primitive worry, without seasoning, and Paris dresses are merely garments for warmth; where people hide their jewels in tree stumps, or attempt to make salad dressing out of motor oil, a France whose present is tragic and whose future is uncertain."

Rolling in with the armies of occupation were portable printing presses, brought to stamp out a new form of currency that would prove devastating to the conquered lands. The new notes, printed on stiff brown paper, were called *Reichskreditkassenscheine*—"military currency certificates," or R.K.K.S., for short. The occupied populations called the currency trooper's money because it was used to pay the salaries of German soldiers serving on occupied soil. Nothing more than promissory notes drawn on German

financial institutions, the money was backed by neither gold nor silver and had no worth other than the power of the military authority to impose its acceptance. But merchants in France, Holland, Belgium, and Scandinavia were compelled to accept it at face value, at a ruinous rate of exchange that was set in Berlin.

The German military paid itself well in trooper's money. In France, according to one estimate, the average German soldier was effectively earning a salary worth fifty times what French soldiers of similar rank on active duty received. German soldiers could not spend these princely wages back home, but in the occupied countries the lowliest private suddenly had the purchasing power of a tycoon. To the Wehrmacht, occupied Europe became one big discount store.

"It seemed as if a dense and never-ending horde of the most destructive type of locust had descended upon Belgium," recalled a Belgian economist, speaking of the German soldiers who swarmed through his country's stores. "Uninterrupted waves of Wehrmacht members emptied the shops of practically everything. The German soldier stole nothing; he paid for his purchases on the dot! The only drawback was that after a few months his greed literally emptied all the shopwindows, counters, and shelves. All of this went into Germany stuffed in the luggage of soldiers on furlough, delighted to bring their wives a few pairs of stockings or their children a brand-new go-cart. From the largest city to the smallest village, long processions of soldiers bending under the weight of their innumerable purchases were a daily sight."

A popular joke was soon making the rounds in Brussels: "Have you heard the latest? Three English spies have just been arrested. They were perfectly disguised as members of the Luftwaffe and spoke German like natives. But the Gestapo caught them anyway. And guess why? Because none of them was carrying even the smallest package!"

The epic shopping spree was of course no laughing matter, for it was not just stockings and go-carts that the Germans bought with their trooper's money. Essential commodities—butter, eggs, meat, and grain—fed the occupiers' garrisons and filled freight trains that were sent steaming straight home to Germany. Suppliers and merchants were left holding crinkly brown-paper assets that were painfully difficult to redeem and that would be completely valueless if Germany should lose the war.

"With these worthless notes, the shelves of stores are being stripped. On average, one store in three is empty and stands with shutters closed," wrote Elizabeth Morrow's correspondent at the end of the summer of 1940. What had happened, the writer continued, amounted to an "invisible form of confiscation. One can call it velvet-glove looting."

Grossly inflated occupation marks, issued by the Germans, gave enormous spending power to Wehrmacht troops, such as the enlisted men shown here buying wine *(top)* in a Belgian shop. At bottom, German soldiers in Paris head for home on leave with a baggage cart laden with booty and pulled by a porter.

Eventually, the *Reichskreditkassenscheine* were phased out, and the occupying forces were paid in local currencies. But that brought no relief to the economies that the occupation bills had helped undermine. The Germans' demand for money proved insatiable, and they sought additional sources of capital. Morrow's friend discovered how thorough the Germans could be in early August, when he and his wife went to their bank to retrieve some railway bonds that had come due. When they arrived, they were told they could open their safe-deposit box only in the presence of a German finance controller and were sent away. Three weeks later they were summoned to reappear at the bank with their keys.

The contents of the safe-deposit box represented their life savings: money and securities earmarked for their children's education and their own retirement. In moments, most of it was gone. The German representative took out everything that could be marketed in a foreign currency— investments in Dutch mines, in General Motors, in General Electric. Then a jeweler weighed and appraised the wife's jewelry and turned it over to the bank manager, to be held "until such time as the Reich shall need it."

The German representative explained: "What is taking place here today is happening in every banking and safe-deposit institution in occupied France. Here is the reason for it. Germany is at present administering France on the basis of an armistice. Eventually the peace terms will be arranged. Among those terms it is certain there will be one requiring the vanquished to pay the victor a cash indemnity."

The stunned couple could barely hear the explanation over the noise of a woman wailing in a nearby cubicle; she had just seen all of her savings vanish into the pocket of another representative of the Reich. Their own treasury official continued, raising his voice: "At the close of the actual war, we do not propose to be hampered by delay, excuse making, or concealment of assets. The contents of safe-deposit boxes and the bank deposits in foreign currency are being added up. We shall have a pretty clear notion of the liquid capital of this country. It will be safe in our hands."

Faced with losing their money in similar fashion, those who had any assets not already in German hands frantically tried to hide what they could. Family silver, jewelry, precious stones, gold coins, stocks and bonds were all tumbled into holes in the ground or stuck among the roots of apple trees. People went to tailors to have the padding removed from the shoulders of their jackets and replaced with packets of bills wrapped in oiled silk. Rings and necklaces were put into boxes of baking soda and epsom salts. One man carefully inserted all of his cash, painstakingly rolled into pencil-size cylinders, into the tubular frame of his typewriter.

The Germans quickly grew wise to the various ruses and took action to

thwart them. Soldiers kept a sharp eye out for suspiciously bumpy rooflines that could indicate fortunes stashed under the tiles. They scanned the surface of the ground for recently turned earth. If they suspected anyone had been digging, they poured water on the place—and dug wherever the wetted soil settled into a depression.

No kind of property was safe. "I have been down to inscribe Lucius and it worries me," confided a French peasant to an acquaintance, after registering his pig with the village clerk in obedience to a German directive ordering a census of farm animals. "I promised my son and his wife a piece of him. I promised my daughter and her husband a piece of him. That makes three families already in that pig. If the whole German army gets in too, where are we?"

The same sort of question was asked by nearly everyone in the summer and the fall of 1940, as all kinds of common supplies ran out and could not be replaced. Soap all but disappeared, and housewives concocted cleaning agents from lye and motor oil mixed with caustic soda—or tried to scrub away grime with the sand bricks formerly used for sharpening knives. New shoes became scarce; the hide of every animal slaughtered in France was reserved for boots for the German army. Stockings were virtually unobtainable; with a good deal of grumbling, reported one Parisian, French women adopted "the barelegged style of American coeds." Private motor transport was all but eliminated; civilian cars that were not confiscated outright had no fuel.

In Denmark, where automobile owners were at least allowed to keep their vehicles, the director of Copenhagen's Carlsbad Brewery made up for the absence of gasoline by hitching a pair of dray horses to his Rolls-Royce, inspiring other Danish car owners to do the same. In other European cities, bicycle riding and rollerskating enjoyed a renaissance. Bicycle taxis, looking like some odd form of western rickshaw, replaced cabs.

The greatest, most pressing shortage was in food. In France, people found themselves juggling several different ration cards for the staples of everyday living: meat, wine, butter, bread, conserves, textiles, and tobacco. But there was no guarantee that commodities governed by rationing would be available from day to day. City dwellers in particular found that obtaining enough to eat could be a full-time job, an onus that gave rise to a new type of work for the elderly and unemployed, the job of "standee." For a small fee, they stood in line to obtain other people's rations—no small task considering that it could easily take five hours or more standing in successive queues to gather the daily allowance for a family of three. Canned goods were not rationed initially, but even so it was impossible to stockpile a supply against a day when they might be. Hoarding was pre-

vented by a simple but effective practice: Grocers would punch a hole in the lid of each can of food as it was sold, thus ensuring that the contents would be used very soon.

Certain foods disappeared almost immediately. Peter de Polnay, a Hungarian writer living in Paris during the early months of occupation, noticed a distinctive pattern in the dwindling of comestibles. "Fats were the first thing to go," he recalled, adding that "Germans chased after butter as a dog chases his tail. Potatoes came next, oil followed. Everything having to do with pork went the same way." Soon signs were appearing in all the grocers' windows: *pas de patates, pas d'huile, pas de porc.* "By the middle of September, Parisians walked to their food shops only to find the laconic notice, *pas de marchandise,*" no merchandise at all.

The German-controlled press brazenly devoted extensive coverage to the shortages, blaming the lack of food and other commodities on the British blockade and accusing the English of deliberately starving the people of Europe. Few but the most ardent German apologists believed what they read. "Look," observed Peter de Polnay and his French friends, playing to the popular stereotype of fat-crazed Germans and their hefty-thighed Fraus. "What's missing? Butter, pork, potatoes, and large-size silk stockings. That speaks for itself."

Nonetheless, the material privations of the occupation—at least in the first year—seemed tolerable. One Frenchman wrote after four months of occupation: "We are not actually hungry, although it would be a positive pleasure to eat more. Nor do I notice any marked change for the worse in the appearance of people whom we meet. Food is short, but one cannot honestly say that we have crossed the line into undernutrition. My children are vigorous, keen for work and fun. People are in the state that an athletic coach would describe as 'trained down a little too fine.'"

Indeed, it was said that the women of Paris had never looked as beautiful as they did in the years of occupation—slimmed down by the lean diet and the constant walking and bicycle riding, still ineffably chic, as only French-women could be, in their simple wartime garb. Cleared of polluting motor vehicles, the great avenues were open to view in all their splendor, the air was pure, and the parks and gardens fragrant. The movie theaters and cabarets remained open, and ancient pastimes such as churchgoing enjoyed a brisk revival. "On Sunday we go to church," wrote Elizabeth Morrow's friend. "Everyone does; it is something to do. The two-mile walk circulates the blood."

While rationing and shortages might all provide grist for humor and the basis for hardy camaraderie, the psychological effects of life in a police state

A cigar-smoking businessman in Copenhagen copes with the gasoline shortage in style, leaving his office for home on a tandem bicycle with his chauffeur pumping the pedals. As fuel restrictions made vehicles unusable, the number of bicycles in Denmark increased from 1.75 to 3.8 million during the first six months of the occupation.

were another matter. For a population that on the whole had enjoyed the freedoms of privacy, unrestricted movement, and open discourse, the all-pervasive control of daily life was nerve-racking. People had to carry documents of all kinds: identity cards, draft cards, labor cards, ration cards. Curfews were imposed, and movement was further restricted by the virtual elimination of civilian transport. Equally restricting was the uncertainty that pervaded daily life. The pretense of normalcy that was provided by leaving native bureaucracies in place merely obscured the extent of German supervision. There was no way to discern what role, power, or degree of control the Germans had kept for themselves. Local governments became unpredictable and arbitrary. Familiar officials who remained in office often behaved uncharacteristically, responding to directives and pressures that were hidden from the people.

The legal system, for instance, followed the familiar forms, but the German police had the authority to alter verdicts. They turned court proceedings into a kind of judicial lottery in which the accused had no way of knowing what type of sentence would be handed down or whether it

Citizens of Grenoble wait in line for handouts from baskets of food provided by Secours national, a French private relief foundation that helped people who had no other means of sustenance.

Submitting to a monthly bureaucratic ordeal, the inhabitants of occupied Oslo queue up to obtain ration cards in the autumn of 1940.

would stand. Defendants actually had reason to fear light sentences, since the Germans were more likely to step in and increase those penalties than they were to intervene when the punishment was more severe.

Even the most scrupulously law-abiding citizen lived under the threat of arrest and arbitrary punishment for minor infractions: violating curfew, blundering into the wrong part of town, uttering a wrong word. All Norway was sickened in December 1940 when word spread of a sixteen-year-old Oslo youth who was picked up for wearing a paper clip—a sign of resistance—in his lapel. He was taken to the headquarters of Quisling's Nazi party, stripped to the waist, and severely beaten.

One day in 1940, Peter de Polnay's cleaning woman arrived at his apartment badly shaken. A friend of hers had been standing in line at the grocer's

that morning when a car full of Germans drew up. As was the practice, the queue stood aside as the Germans entered the store. When they emerged some time later carrying large parcels, the grocer closed his door and hung out the all-too-familiar *pas de marchandise* sign. *"Sales Boches,"* muttered the charwoman's friend, expressing a common curse—"Dirty Germans." Within moments, two plainclothesmen arrived and pushed their way into the cluster of shoppers still lingering in front of the store. They carted the terrified woman off to a German billet, forced her to clean 500 pairs of boots, and told her that next time she slurred the Germans she would go to prison.

By the end of the year it seemed that everyone in occupied Europe had heard dozens of such stories, although few details were forthcoming in the German-controlled press. Communication of news by press, radio, or cinema was rigorously supervised. Often the only available source of uncensored information was the smudged circulars of the clandestine press. They showed up everywhere, but as one Frenchman put it, were "more dangerous than copperheads to have on the premises." Mail was censored and in some cases prohibited entirely. The only private written communication permitted between the residents of occupied and nonoccupied France was printed postcards bearing multiple-choice messages such as "We are well/ill." The sender conveyed his own message by crossing out the parts that did not apply.

The policy of the established press was to print nothing that could be construed as unfavorable to Germany, and penalties for violating the prac-

German soldiers check the identification cards of bicyclists crossing the border between Vichy and occupied France. Any French person over the age of fifteen who failed to produce the required card with fingerprints was liable to imprisonment.

A sneering Frenchman in a Fascist uniform grabs the hat from the head of a fellow Parisian who has refused to stand during the passage of a Fascist parade down the Champs-Élysées in 1943. Tensions between pro-German and anti-German factions in France surfaced more and more as the occupation wore on.

tice were severe—even in the relatively lightly ruled "model protectorate," Denmark. Several months after the Germans' arrival there, Gunnar Helweg-Larsen, editor of the *Kristeligt Dagblad* in Copenhagen, printed a story about a certain small forest in Denmark that was infested by a particularly voracious species of grub. He included some choice pieces of scientific information gleaned from an encyclopedia about the parasite, which, as it happened, originated in Prussia. Apparently there was no known means of eliminating it. But if nature took its course, the grub would devour everything in the wood, then die of hunger. The following year the wood would be as fresh and green as before. The analogy was inescapable, and Helweg-Larsen was relieved of his job.

The stranglehold the Germans maintained on all channels of communication produced an indescribable sense of disorientation and isolation. "You had to have been in occupied France to understand what people felt in the hermetically sealed German coffin," wrote Peter de Polnay. Elizabeth Morrow's friend wrote of the spiritual withering caused by the absence of free discourse and the dearth of factual news. "Subtly, skillfully, and imperceptibly, like a transfusion of blood, Germany is modifying the stream of thought that circulates through the French mind. Hardly conscious of what is being done to her, France is the victim of a news conditioning and an idea conditioning that is affecting the intellectual atmosphere precisely as air conditioning affects the temperature of a building." After spending some time in Paris, he wrote, "The apathy of the crowd that filters into the boulevards is anything but French. It is unnatural, foreboding, deadly."

German soldiers were beginning to find Paris fairly deadly too. "I'd always heard that Paris is the gayest city in the world, a city where you can have a wonderful time. But I must say I thought it was the gloomiest city in the world," wrote the Luftwaffe flight sergeant Gottfried Leske in his diary after visiting Paris on leave in November 1940. "All the people walk around with grim, unpleasant faces," he complained, going on to criticize the quality of French food and lambaste the French people for their own complaints about coal shortages and food lines. "They seem to think that's something unbelievably awful," he sneered. "After all, nothing happened to them. I mean, they weren't even bombed." According to Leske, even the fabled prostitutes of the City of Light did not measure up to their reputation. "All in all, Paris is disappointing. Awfully disappointing."

For many other German soldiers, Paris in the winter of 1940-41 was worse than disappointing. It had actually become threatening. With the failure of the Luftwaffe to win the Battle of Britain that autumn, the German military was looking far less invincible than it had the previous spring, and the civilian population was getting tired of the pervasive *feldgrau*, the field gray of the German uniform. Tempers on both sides frayed. The German pose of correctness evaporated, and the occupied Europeans became more and more resentful. Germans were given poor service in restaurants and increasingly snubbed on the streets. Occasionally, it was claimed, potshots were taken at them.

"Stories of German soldiers being shot were all over the town," recalled Peter de Polnay—who tended to regard most of the tales skeptically. However, one night while sitting at his local bar, he observed a German soldier, who obviously was ready to leave, linger on conspicuously. The man slowly put on his coat and hat, then stood irresolutely at the door. Finally, too afraid to walk outside alone, he asked the barman to accompany him to his car, which was outside on the square.

By 1941, German promises for the future of Europe were proving to be empty ones. The conquest had been presented as the prelude to the creation of a new European community that would integrate the econo-

mies of industrial and agricultural countries and free them from their dependence on overseas suppliers. Theoretically, this scheme put western Europeans on an equal footing with their German partners. As Hitler's press chief, Otto Dietrich, put it in 1941, what he called the "spiritual foundations" of the new Europe would result in a "racially constituted but organically combined ordering of nations."

But by then the open economic exploitation of western Europe had made it abundantly evident that behind the rhetoric of European unity lay a different reality—one more accurately expressed by Hitler's privately stated aim to come out of the war "bursting with fat!" Even the most ardent supporters of a European economic community could see that when Hitler spoke of Europe, he meant a Greater German Empire in which the occupied people were relegated to an inferior status that ensured they would live in permanent want.

As if to dramatize the situation, the winter of 1940-41 came early and was one of Europe's coldest in decades; Paris suffered seventy days of below-freezing temperatures. Heating oil was unobtainable, and coal became the most treasured of commodities; people tramped over dumps and along railroad tracks to glean the precious single lumps. Some resorted to papier-mâché for fuel or attempted to heat their homes with sawdust packed into old paint cans and burned in wood stoves.

Pictures of German officers adorn a copy of the *Illustrierter Beobachter*, a German journal being hawked by a Parisian newsboy in 1940. The official French press printed only news from German-controlled bureaus, but by 1944 more than 1,200 underground presses were spreading the anti-Nazi message throughout France.

A French periodical summed up a few of the tricks people used to keep warm: "The best solution is to stay in bed wearing a pair of fur gloves, a polo-necked sweater, even the kind of nightcap the smart designers are already proposing. The Sunday stroll that used to end in a cinema or a museum now leads nowhere except a bench deep down in the metro, in the warm bosom of the earth. Some make for hospitals, or botanical greenhouses and the monkey house at the zoo. Others find nowhere better than the lobbies of banks."

Life did not improve much with the arrival of warm weather. Indeed, as a whole, it worsened following the German invasion of the Soviet Union in June. Germany had expected to win the war quickly. But when the

following winter arrived and the army in the east stalled in the Russian snows, it was clear that the days of blitzkrieg were over. Germany was now committed to a protracted war that would drain its manpower and resources for months to come. Its need to increase arms production and obtain goods that it could no longer make for itself led to stepped-up demands on the occupied countries and hence to corresponding hardships for their civilian populations.

"Food was the single overriding obsession of those years," recalled Gilles Perrault, a Paris schoolboy during the occupation. "Food haunted the imagination from morning till night. And then at night we dreamed about it." Another Parisian recalled an evening at the movies when an old film featuring a banquet scene was played. When the table full of food appeared on the screen the audience stood up and cheered.

The scarcity of food was exacerbated by problems with the transportation system. Because of the chronic shortages of fuel, rubber, and rolling stock, the little food that was available often was not distributed at all, or spoiled while waiting on the siding for transport. Diets became increasingly vegetarian. For many of those who lived in cities, the only available meat came from a sorry assortment of urban animals: pigeons netted in parks, rabbits raised on rooftops, or—for those in very small apartments—guinea pigs nicknamed flat-dwellers' rabbits. So many cats disappeared from the streets and into cooking pots that an official warning was issued against the dangers of feline stew. "Cat eaters—attention!" read a notice in the Paris

Norwegians in the district of Hardanger stage a mock funeral procession—complete with violinist and horse-drawn "hearse"—to deliver newly banned radios to occupation officials in November of 1943. Opposite, complying with the same decree, Norwegians elsewhere lug their radios into a German collection center.

papers on October 31, 1941. The text explained that because cats ate disease-bearing rats, their bodies harbored dangerous bacilli that posed a serious threat to humans. The warning had little effect. The hunger was so great that the traffic in cat meat continued to flourish.

By 1942, most of the occupied populations were living on two-thirds to half of their prewar calories. Children were so undernourished that their growth was impaired. A 1944 survey of fourteen-year-olds in one of the poorest sections of Paris found that the boys were nearly three inches shorter, and the girls more than four inches shorter, than the average heights for their age. A report prepared by the medical department of a Flemish relief agency commented that the national diet in Belgium was "the lowest and most inadequate ever imposed on a large mass of people for a prolonged period."

The effects of chronic malnourishment rippled though society. Industrial accidents increased, and the natural resistance to disease weakened. The rate of illness rose, and infectious disease reached epidemic proportions—at a time when few drugs were available to fight back. Tuberculosis became more prevalent; in Paris it killed twice as many people during the occupation as it had before the war. In 1943, polio swept through Holland; a year later a virulent strain of diphtheria raged through the country. In all of the occupied countries, the poor, the elderly, and the infirm were the hardest hit. By January 1942, the mortality rate in Paris was 46 percent higher than the average for the years from 1932 through 1938; postwar estimates attributed 150,000 French deaths directly to malnutrition.

One way to fend off starvation was to supplement legal rations with black market supplies costing ten to twelve times the official price. But because salaries on the whole remained at their prewar levels, most people were hard-pressed to come up with the money for black market foodstuffs. A 1943 survey of 2,729 wage-earning French families found that they had an average of 876 francs a month per family member—the price of four and a half pounds of butter on the black market. An estimated 71 percent of the average

Parisian budget was spent on food. Other black market commodities also cut deeply into family budgets. In Belgium, a toothbrush cost 23 times what it had before the war; a cotton shirt, 1,400 times more. Soap went for 85 to 90 times its prewar price; dishrags and clothes starch were from 20 to 40 times as expensive as they had been.

Poverty spread and with it came associated social ills—child neglect and crime among them. The once notably law-abiding Netherlands saw its crime rate triple in 1942. In some areas, prostitution increased by as much as tenfold as a result of financial hardship. By far the most common crime was black market trafficking. In 1942, French peasants sold well over a third of their butter, eggs, and pigs on the black market. A quarter of all the potatoes and half of all the chickens went the same way. In 1943, 1,150,000 tons of meat were slaughtered in France; only 191,000 tons reached the legal market. The illegal trade was so pervasive, wrote the Belgian economist Raoul Miry, that in his country it assumed "the character of a national institution, spontaneously created beyond the law by the tacit but effective consent of all citizens, great and small, rich and poor, regardless of class or profession."

The effect of the underground economy was to increase shortages and add to the hardships of the majority, which was forced to spend meager resources to buy necessities at wildly inflated prices. At the same time, the handful who could afford the price lived royally. German officers, collaborators, and high-rolling black-marketeers stuffed themselves at the table, reported the French writer Jean Galtier-Boissière bitterly after dining out one evening at a fashionable Paris restaurant. "The room was crowded," he wrote in his diary. "An enormous Fritz who, it seems, was Lieutenant Weber, *Führer* of the Franco-German press, was treating his friends to champagne. No restrictions: Forbidden beefsteaks were hidden under fried eggs. The finest wines flowing. Fat cats are on top in the New Order. With cash, plenty of cash, one can always stuff one's face as much as one likes, while housewives stand in the snow for turnips."

Beyond the preoccupation with food, the extensive material shortages of occupation, coupled with the other exigencies of war, altered the patterns of daily existence in other ways. Life grew increasingly family-centered as travel became more difficult and blackouts and curfews kept people at home. Living quarters became more crowded as networks of relatives shared homes because of evacuations and a growing housing shortage; in the winter, many families lived in a single room to take best advantage of the available heat.

"There was no question of getting away at weekends," recalled the

Taking advantage of scarcity in a wartime winter, profiteers wait at a Brussels trolley stop with bundles of goods destined for the black market.

Parisian Gilles Perrault. "To invite friends for dinner without asking them for food tickets was to sacrifice the family's vital nourishment. So we stayed at home, among ourselves. Some people played interminable card games. Reading became prodigiously popular. Muffled in layers of woolens, with our gloves on, we read from nightfall, windows shuttered against a hostile world. Any book printed sold right out and there were an enormous number published (in 1943, as many in France as in Britain and the United States combined), but still not enough because paper was in short supply. People borrowed more and more voraciously from the municipal libraries; booksellers on the banks of the Seine looked on while people snapped up all their old junk."

People everywhere in Europe eagerly seized upon distractions. In Hol-

land, as in France, there was a boom in the sale of books, particularly historical and travel literature and textbooks. And even though the variety and quality of commercial entertainment had declined, attendance at movies and athletic events in the Netherlands doubled from 1941 to 1943.

On the whole, such diversions offered only minor relief from the daily grind and petty humiliations that made life steadily more depressing and stress-ridden as time wore on. "The streets fill with automatons," wrote the French diarist Alfred Fabre-Luce. "Frail shoulders are bowed down under the burden of parcels and suitcases; old men ride secondhand bicycles, their bodies rigid, their expression anxious, their hands gripping the handlebars as though they were accomplishing a heroic performance. Those who have no leverage whatsoever and have nothing to barter with must learn to be humble in the extreme. When one has to spend several hours in line, filling in forms, getting the paperwork together, signing that one is not Jewish, one does not recover one's self-respect any too quickly."

For the hapless Jews themselves, what passed for ordinary life was even more difficult. The repressive anti-Jewish measures enacted in all the occupied countries both magnified the hardships of day-to-day existence and all but eliminated the few distractions that helped make life endurable. Writing in her diary on June 20, 1942, thirteen-year-old Anne Frank rattled off the long list of anti-Jewish regulations then in force in Amsterdam: "Jews must wear a yellow star, Jews must hand in their bicycles, Jews are banned from trams and are forbidden to drive. Jews are only allowed to do their shopping between three and five o'clock and then only in shops which bear the placard 'Jewish shop.' Jews must be indoors by eight o'clock and cannot even sit in their own gardens after that hour. Jews are forbidden to visit theatres, cinemas and other places of entertainment. Jews may not take part in public sports. Swimming baths, tennis courts, hockey fields and other sports grounds are all prohibited to them. Jews may not visit Christians. Jews must go to Jewish schools, and many more restrictions of a similar kind."

Four days later she wrote wearily: "It is boiling hot, we are all positively melting, and in this heat I have to walk everywhere. Now I can fully appreciate how nice a tram is; but that is a forbidden luxury for Jews—shank's mare is good enough for us."

Janet Tesissier Du Cros, the wife of a French scientist, recounted one small, pathetic incident that dramatized the difference between her life and that of the Jews: "I was standing in an interminable queue in front of a stall where there were cabbages for sale. The weather was cold and damp, and the long queue of weary people moved very slowly forward. Suddenly a little old woman with the yellow star on her thin black coat came humbly

forward and stood hesitating on the edge of the pavement. Jews were not allowed to stand in queues. What they were supposed to do, I never discovered. But the moment the people in the queue saw her, they signed to her to join us. Secretly and rapidly, as in a game of hunt-the-slipper, she was passed up until she stood at the head of the queue. I am glad to say that not one voice was raised in protest, that the policeman standing near turned his head away, and that she got her cabbage before any of us."

Sadly, few Jews in Europe in those years could count on such kindness or consideration. The same rules that made life so excessively difficult for them also thoroughly isolated them from their countrymen. While many Gentiles privately pitied the Jews, few dared risk the repercussions of extending even a modest helping hand. Indeed, non-Jews were likely to react to scenes of persecution with the coolness and hostility that another Jewish Frenchwoman encountered on the day she and her children were arrested by the Paris police. "We went out of the house, me pushing the pram and the four children holding on to me tightly, frightened and ashamed of being led away by policemen. On our clothes we were wearing the yellow star. People stared at us. I don't know what they were thinking. Their expressions were empty, apparently indifferent. A woman started shouting, 'Well done! Well done! They can all go to hell.' The children huddled against me."

Up through 1941 it was unclear where all the repressive measures against the Jews were leading. Even in Hitler's inner circle, much of the long-term planning for western Europe's Jews still centered around shipping them to overseas reservations. But in July 1941, the SS Security Service chief, Reinhard Heydrich, started work on the plan that he presented the following January to a ministerial conference in the Berlin suburb of Wannsee. Heydrich's "Final Solution" called for total elimination of the European Jews by systematically shipping them out of the occupied western countries to death camps in the east.

By the spring of 1942, the trains of cattle cars were hauling the pitiful cargo out from every corner of occupied Europe. By June, when Anne Frank was still fretting about her grades in school, the mass deportations of her Jewish countrymen were well under way. By the end of the year, 40,000 Dutch Jews had been shipped out—ostensibly for jobs in Germany, in reality for hard labor and then extermination at Auschwitz. Nearly 42,000 Jews had been sent to the death camps from France, and 15,000 from Belgium.

Their fate was not known for certain, but rumors quickly began to filter through to the West. In July 1942, the former Polish prime minister Stanislaw Mikolajczyk, from exile in London, provided details of the death

camps in a radio speech. The reports were largely discounted as war propaganda, although hundreds of Jewish families were sufficiently alarmed to go into hiding.

Many more Jews, still unaware that for them Europe was now a giant deathtrap, continued to obey the laws scrupulously, hoping that by so doing they could ride out the occupation. The Rosenblums, a Polish family that had moved to Paris in 1930, were typical. When the French police knocked on their door on July 16, 1942, the first night of Paris's *Grande Rafle*—the "Big Roundup" that swept up 12,884 Jews—the Rosenblums were given three hours to prepare for what they were told would be a brief trip to inspect their papers. The family obediently, unhesitatingly com-

A Jewish girl leaving the deportation camp at Westerbork in the Netherlands, en route to probable death, peers forlornly from a railroad car *(above)*. By 1943, at locations like Westerbork *(right)*, Jews were regularly loaded onto freight cars destined for the extermination camps in eastern Europe.

plied. "My parents were very religious, observant; they were people of great probity," recalled Gitla Rosenblum, who was ten years old at the time. "They had done nothing wrong, and there was nothing to reproach them with. So they stayed, got dressed, and prepared a small bundle. My father went to the synagogue to fetch a scroll, the Torah, which a pious Jew ought to have on him if he is going away."

When the gendarmes returned, the Rosenblums were taken to a collection area, loaded onto buses, and driven to the outskirts of Paris to join the wretched crowd gathered at the Vélodrome d'Hiver sports arena. Eight days later, the stadium was emptied, and all the inmates were transferred in cattle trucks to the deportation camps at Pithiviers, Beaune-la-Rolande, and Drancy that over the next three years would serve as France's threshold to extermination.

The Rosenblums were taken to Pithiviers, where Gitla's father and brother were immediately removed to another part of the camp. Several weeks

later, Gitla and five-year-old Sarah were separated from their mother and older sister. Gitla caught one last glimpse of her family as they left Pithiviers, her father and brother, like the other men, with their heads shaved. "That was the departure for Auschwitz. I can see the roll call of the crowd. My father had worn a beard. It had been shaved too—it was an atrocious sight. They were taken off in transports whose destination nobody knew. Not one of them came back."

Gitla and Sarah were transferred to the camp at Drancy, joining other children who had already seen their families deported. All through July and into August 1942, 4,000 Jewish children—from infancy to twelve years old, most already unknowingly orphaned by the Final Solution—were gathered at Drancy, "dumped from buses in the middle of the courtyard as if they were little beasts," recalled an inmate who saw the pitiful consignments arrive. In panic, they cried inconsolably. Camp officials vainly tried to impose some order on the chaos, attempting to list the children by name before consigning them to the trains for transport. But many of the children were too young to know their own names; they were entered on the train lists as question marks. Those old enough to actually realize that they were going to be sent somewhere invented a name for their destination: "Pitchipoi."

A Red Cross social worker named Annette Monod helped a seven-year-old write a last letter to the only person he knew who was still alive, the concierge of his apartment house: "Madame la Concierge. I am writing to

Inmates of the Drancy deportation camp in France do their washing and cleaning at an outdoor trough *(opposite)*. As many as sixty people were crowded into each room *(below)* of the quarters at Drancy. Some 70,000 Jews passed through the squalid camps between the summers of 1941 and 1944.

you because I have nobody else. Last week, Papa was deported. Mama was deported. I have lost my purse. I have nothing left."

Later, Monod stayed with her young charges as a group of them were gathered up to be led to the train. A gendarme tried to have a roll call. But the children, she wrote, did not understand what was expected of them and did not answer when their names were called. Some of the smaller ones wandered away from the crowd. One small boy approached a gendarme, attracted by his shiny whistle; a little girl ambled over to an embankment to pick some flowers. Finally the police gave up, abandoning the roll call in favor of a head count to ensure that the day's quota was filled.

Fighting back her tears, Monod accompanied the group to the train station. Each child carried a little bundle of belongings. "The place where we were was only about 200 meters from the station. But the distance was made no shorter for these tots by their awkward bundles. That was when I saw a gendarme carry the miserable package belonging to a wisp of a boy of four or five, for him to be better able to walk. But a warrant officer objected, bawling out the gendarme on the grounds that a Frenchman in uniform does not carry the package of a Jew. Crestfallen, the gendarme gave the child back his package. I followed the column, my heart aching, unable to turn my back on these little children who had been in my care for only a few weeks."

When the group reached the departure platform, Monod noticed that a German sentry standing on a passageway above the station had covered the children with his machine gun. "Getting onto the train then took place with an anxiety that had turned feverish. The freight cars had no footboards, and many of the children were too small to step up. The bigger ones climbed in first and then helped pull in the smaller ones. The gendarmes lent a hand, taking the youngest, still babies in arms, and passing them up to those already inside." Then the children, realizing that they were about to leave, succumbed to fear. They began to sob, and called out to the social workers and even the gendarmes to help them.

Monod recalled that one child, a five-year-old boy, began to whimper that he had to go to the bathroom. "Begging for my help, he called out, 'I want to get down, I want to see the lady again, I don't want to do peepee here, I want the lady to help me.'" As the door of the wagon was closed and padlocked, the weeping child reached his hand imploringly out through a crack between two planks and continued to cry out to Monod. Then the warrant officer hit the hand, and it disappeared into the wagon.

Gitla and Sarah Rosenblum were spared that child's piteous fate through luck and the desperate string pulling of an uncle who, because he had been classified as an "economically valuable" worker in the fur trade, was still

Having been released from internment camps in Vichy France, children smile in the summer sun in 1943 at a home for Jewish youngsters in the French town of Izieux. The following spring, on Gestapo orders, all forty-four residents of the home were deported and gassed, along with six of their guardians.

free. The two girls were released, taken to the unoccupied zone, and placed with a peasant family who was paid to look after them by one of the charitable organizations then working tirelessly to save Jewish children.

Over the next three years, as more than 75,000 Jews of all ages were deported from France, shattering scenes such as the one Annette Monod later recalled with such clarity became commonplace. Jewish children were hidden all over France, much as stocks and bonds and family silver had earlier been tumbled into wells and shoved under roof tiles. Some of the children were taken into peasant households; others found refuge in orphanages set up in the relative safety of the unoccupied zone.

But by the autumn of 1943, after German occupation had been extended to all of France, even the most discreet of these havens became precarious. As each month passed and it became more apparent that they would lose the war, the Germans seemed to be venting their rage on the civilian population in a kind of frenzy. The occupiers had long ago stripped off the velvet glove in dealing with their western satellites, but now the terrorism became increasingly random and arbitrary. The tentacles of labor conscription reached further into society, ever harsher reprisal measures were taken for acts of resistance, and the campaign against the Jews intensified.

In the spring of 1944, the Gestapo chief of Lyons, Klaus Barbie, already notorious as the torturer of martyred Resistance leader Jean Moulin, began ordering the summary execution of the prisoners under his control. Then, on April 6, as if deliberately seeking out new victims, he ordered the closing

of a small children's home in the nearby village of Izieux. Forty-four Jewish children, along with adult social workers, were taken the next day to Drancy; within weeks all of them with the exception of one social worker had been gassed at Auschwitz.

As the atrocities mounted, anyone who still had a radio listened intently to BBC broadcasts, excitedly sensing the impending Allied landing from the flood of "personal messages" transmitted to the Resistance. "We listened religiously to these enigmatic fragments of weighty baroque poetry," recalled Gilles Perrault. " 'The moon is full of green elephants' may well have referred to airborne operations, but 'Venus has a pretty navel,' 'The hippo is not carnivorous,' 'Thérèse is always sleepy'? Without being able to make head or tail of them, we assumed it meant that something was happening.

"And then we trustingly thought that they would come because we just could not go on any longer. There was absolutely nothing left. We had thought we had reached the end so many times, yet the finish line kept moving farther back. Supplies ran out. Rail and road links were cut one after the other by Allied planes. Vegetables disappeared from the markets. Cooking posed a problem because gas was available only at mealtimes, and then there was hardly any of it. Power cuts were incessant. Half the metro stations were permanently closed. Feverishly the enemy increased roundups. You had only to be caught outside the cinema without your papers to be bundled without a trial into a cattle truck headed for Germany."

Then, on Tuesday morning, June 6, Perrault saw three windows flung open simultaneously on his street. Two women and a man yelled in unison, "The English have landed."

As thrilling as that was, Paris still lived in fear of the retaliatory frenzy of Germany in its death throes. Fully retaining their capacity for destruction, the Germans set fire to buildings and kept up the massacre of prisoners. Only days after the Allied landing, the city was shocked and sobered after learning by word of mouth about the horrifying destruction of the village of Oradour-sur-Glane and the massacre of its entire population of 639—all in retaliation for the death of a single Waffen-SS officer.

Moreover, the ever-present food shortages finally reached famine levels. All of the capital's provisions were now being ferried into the city in a few dozen trucks that faced constant peril from Allied bombers. Each truck carried a white flag and a pair of lookouts lying supine on the front fenders. Each lookout held one end of a piece of string in his hand; the other end was attached to the driver's arm. At the sight of a plane, a tug on the string signaled the driver to slam on the brakes—often sending his vehicle careening into a ditch. Losses were so frequent that volunteers became

Left homeless by the fighting in 1944, French refugees bed down on straw in the cathedral of the heavily bombed city of Caen, with little but prayer for protection from the war swirling around them.

scarcer by the day, further constricting the food supply. "We were starving. We had been saying that for four years, but the menus of 1943 now appeared positively sumptuous."

But Paris was even then on the eve of her own late-summer liberation. Elsewhere, whole populations still had a terrible winter to endure. Toward the end of that final year, the editor of a German newspaper, returning defensively to the hoary theme of European unity, wrote: "We did not cross our frontiers in order to subdue other peoples in a blind madness for conquest. We came as heralds of a new order and a new justice."

Yet all around, Nazi Germany's true epitaph had already been indelibly carved into the shattered countries that had endured five brutally transforming years of occupation. ✚

Scorched Earth in Norway

On October 28, 1944, Adolf Hitler ordered the wholesale devastation of Norway's Finnmark region to slow the Russian pursuit of the Wehrmacht forces as they withdrew from the area. For the inhabitants of Finnmark (*inset, opposite*), the northernmost part of Norway, Hitler's edict could not have come at a worse time. Already, sub-zero temperatures heralded winter's onslaught and the tundra bristled with frost. Any citizen choosing to stay would, in the words of German Reichskommissar Josef Terboven, expose "himself and his family to possible death in the Arctic without house or food."

The job of purging Finnmark fell to Germany's Twentieth Mountain Army. Since September, the 200,000-man force had been preparing to retreat from the salients that they had driven into Russian territory. A series of stunning reversals for the Wehrmacht elsewhere in the east had at last persuaded Hitler to withdraw his overextended army farther into occupied Norway. To prevent the pursuing Soviets from gaining a foothold in Finnmark, Hitler ordered the army's commanding general, Lothar Rendulic, to remove the people and burn the land behind his retreating troops.

Under Rendulic's command, special army demolition squads swept through Finnmark's villages, driving terrified residents from their homes, torching buildings, slaughtering livestock for the army's use, and scattering precious provisions to the wind. Thousands of Finnmark's inhabitants were deported south aboard confiscated Norwegian fishing vessels and trucks, or were forced to march alongside the withdrawing army.

Thousands more residents fled to the countryside; some sought refuge in mines and caves, while others later returned to cobble primitive shelters from the charred wreckage of their towns. All told, Rendulic's soldiers razed 11,000 houses, 116 schools, 27 churches, and 21 hospitals. By late December, the general boasted that only about 200 Norwegians remained in Finnmark. He would not rest, he vowed, until even those few were deported.

German patrol boats heave to in the background as frightened

Norwegian
Sea

North Cape

Barents
Sea

SOROY I.

Gamvik

Berlevag

NORWAY

Tromso

FINNMARK

Vadso

Varanger Fjord

Kirkenes

Petsamo

Narvik

U.S.S.R.

SWEDEN

FINLAND

0   50   100   150 mi

0   50 100 150 km

F18HV

civilians from Norway's Finnmark await deportation south aboard a commandeered Norwegian fishing boat.

German military guards shepherd Finnmark deportees aboard a fishing vessel. During their coastal journey south, exiles endured fierce cold, dreadful sanitation, and the constant threat of attack by Soviet submarines.

With little more than the coats on their backs, evacuees leave a German truck for transfer to a boat. The displaced residents, many of them old, faced an uncertain future in evacuation camps located in territory under German occupation.

Fugitives from German deportation squads clamber up a snowy slope on the island of Soroy in northern Finnmark. Such escapees braved months of extreme privation in Arctic wilderness hideouts.

A Swath of Destruction

From improvised shelters deep in the hills, Norwegians in hiding watched as General Rendulic's army transformed Finnmark's villages into islands of flame. With terrible efficiency, the retreating Germans worked their way west, laying a hundred-mile swath of devastation from Kirkenes to Vadso on Finnmark's Varanger Fjord by early November.

From there they proceeded north to the port of Berlevag. A

Norwegian recalled the utter desolation of that town in the wake of the army: "Not a single house remained. Those who had not been carried off by the Germans had hidden in the mountains. Only seventy people were left. We found them searching among the ruins for a can of food or a piece of timber."

Even after the Arctic snows had smothered the town's last fire, the terror lingered. German raiding parties returned to flush out fugitives, level half-standing walls, and kill livestock that had survived the initial slaughter. The Norwegians countered the Germans' thoroughness with an iron resolve to remain in Finnmark's ruined land.

Under a pall of black smoke, a German demolition unit prepares to raze another section of the port of Vadso. Rushing to outpace their Soviet pursuers, the Germans succeeded in leveling only 70 percent of the town before moving on.

Residents of Berlevag who escaped deportation return to the smoldering wreckage of their once-prosperous coastal village. They carry fish, the only food to be had in the new wasteland.

A child in the fishing village of Gamvik stands beside a shelter fashioned from the overturned hull of a boat. The makeshift dwelling housed eight people, two cows, and a goat.

Clinging to the Land

The Germans charged with evacuating Finnmark's towns did not anticipate the stubborn fortitude of the people. Undaunted by imponderable loss, and with winter hard upon them, these stalwart survivors clung to their land: Thousands blended into the rocky hills to await the Germans' passage, returning days later to their leveled towns to live in gutted basements or mud huts. There, plagued by disease and wrenching cold, they subsisted on salt fish, whale fat, and what little flour happened to be left.

Others, fearful of returning raiders, chose to stay in the caves and caverns that had concealed them so well. Some remained in their mountain hideaways until, by chance, Norwegian rescue parties discovered them at war's end.

Occupants of the boat house above had to rely on their own body heat and the warmth of a lantern to ward off the chill of the icy sea winds.

Deliverance from the Terror

First among Finnmark's populace to be liberated were the inhabitants of Kirkenes, a mining village on the region's eastern border. In mid-October 1944, as the retreating German army pressed into Finnmark, 4,000 townspeople had sought haven from the rampaging troops in the dank tunnels of a nearby mine.

From their underground refuge, Kirkenes's terrified residents listened to the staccato bursts of shellfire. The din continued for several days as the German rear guard held off the advancing Russians.

Finally, word reached the enclave of exiles: The Red Army had reached Kirkenes. For the refugees huddled in the mine, the German reign of terror was at an end.

Under the Norwegian flag, joyful residents of Kirkenes stream out of the Bjornevatn iron mine where, a week before, they had taken refuge from the German army. Liberating Soviet troops greet them on the left.

The Hardest Winter

Even before the north wind began to strip leaves from the elms, the Dutch sensed that they faced a terrible irony: Knowing that peace was soon to come, the Allied world cheered as bombers destroyed Germany's industrial capacity and watched avidly as immense armies clenched a fist around Berlin. Yet even as the Third Reich crumbled, the rag-clad Dutch were starving in the frigid embrace of the war's final winter.

The people of the occupied Netherlands huddled in the bitter cold as the rescuers from the West charged past their country and penetrated ever deeper into the German heartland. The Allied failure to capture the bridge over the Rhine at Arnhem delayed liberation indefinitely. Dutch morale sank further under the knowledge that the loss of their railway system—which they themselves had shut down under orders from their government-in-exile—had only made their situation worse. Furthermore, the German occupiers, whose leaders had cherished the notion that they were being considerate to the racially acceptable Dutch,

now dropped all pretense of civility. Having already pillaged the country of everything of material value, the desperate German troops began seizing food, and soon starvation descended on the Dutch people. In Rotterdam alone, deaths from starvation averaged 400 a day. In all, 18,000 Dutch died of hunger and related diseases before spring and German surrender brought relief.

But rescue did not seem a foregone conclusion. One could die while waiting for it. "Like thousands of others, I ate sugar beets and dried tulip bulbs," wrote Henri van der Zee, who was only ten years old at the time. "I had hardly any clothes and no shoes at all; I saw people being dragged away or hiding in fear; and I witnessed cruelty and violence at their worst."

Supplies grew more and more scarce. Both the Allies and the Germans had blown up dikes, flooding villages and fields of crops. Meager rations had to be stretched even further. But the valiant Dutch people endured. As van der Zee added, "I also witnessed friendship and sacrifice at their best."

Dutch rationing coupons were of little use when no food was available in the stores.

His legs reduced to sticks, a Dutch boy gazes longingly into a shopwindow. The sign advertises only scouring powder, itself a rare commodity.

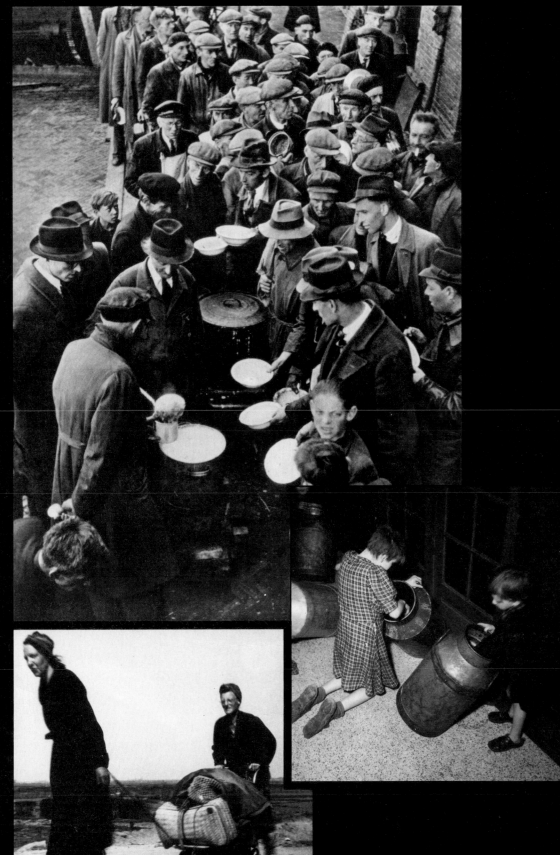

Bowls in hand, hungry men crowd around an outdoor soup kitchen, whose offering was likely to be no more than a watery broth of unpeeled potatoes. At another such kitchen, two children *(far right)* scrape the dregs from food canisters.

Two women in search of food show the strain as they struggle to move a heavily laden perambulator across the frozen land. The more fortunate had bicycles, with which they could forage over wide areas. As food grew even more scarce, barter became the norm: bracelets for butter, tools for potatoes and eggs.

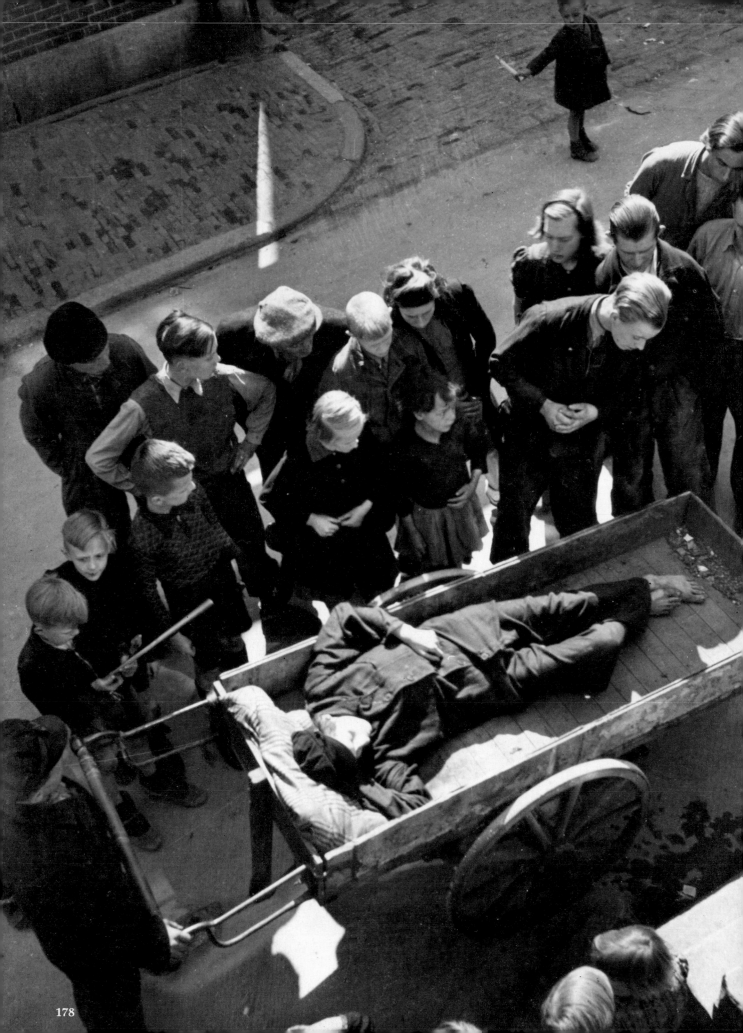

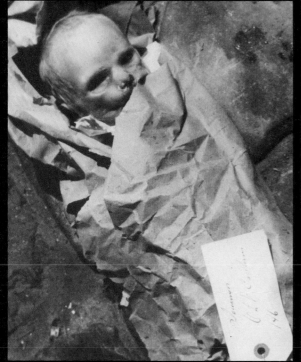

The corpse of an infant lies wrapped in a shroud of rough paper. With little wood available for coffins, the dead were often buried in paper or cardboard.

Bodies long overdue for burial wait their turn on the floor of a church. Lacking dray horses, the Dutch often teamed up to pull the hearses to the graveyards.

Daily Images of the Dead and Dying

As the winter wore on, disease and death became rampant, choosing in particular the very young and the very old as victims. By February, the Dutch were dying at a rate five times that of September—so rapidly that their bodies were stacked up along the roadsides or stretched out in churches to await burial. The vast number of deaths in Amsterdam overwhelmed the city's undertakers. "We were lucky it was such a cold winter," a city official recalled. "It prevented the bodies from decomposing too quickly and causing epidemics."

A father rescues his children
from Wieringermeer Polder
(opposite), whose villages and
cropland were inundated after
the Germans mined its dikes.

Anticipating retreat but lacking
transport, German troops seize
bicycles from the Dutch at the
Royal Palace in Amsterdam.

Nazi Raids
and Reprisals

In the waning months of the war,
German measures against the
Dutch grew more and more harsh.
Raids increased in frequency and
ferocity. House-to-house searches
flushed out suspected Resistance
members, who were deported to
work camps or shot. Then, with
many of Holland's polders already
flooded, the Nazis started mining
the nation's remaining dikes in
preparation for a last-ditch stand.
In April, they blew up the great
polder of Wieringermeer, rendering
thousands of people homeless.

Jubilant Dutch plunge across wet fields to harvest airborne food *(opposite)*. Though famished, the people cooperated in an orderly distribution.

Beside themselves with joy, Dutch women rush toward food falling from an Allied aircraft.

Relief from the Sky

As April brought the thaw and an end to tedious Allied-German talks on allowing mercy flights over Holland, British and American planes at last began delivering food to designated drop zones. The relief effort, Operation Manna, sent more than 7,000 tons of food tumbling down to hordes of hungry Dutch.

For the thousands who might not have survived another day, the first day of the drop evoked immeasurable emotion. An onlooker in The Hague recalled hearing the first of the Lancaster bombers: "We raced outside, waved with hats, shawls, flags, sheets, with anything, to the planes which by now were thundering over our streets. In a flash our whole quiet street was filled with a cheering, waving crowd, and the elated people were even dancing on their roofs."

Within days all Holland was free. The winter of hunger melted away, but the sorrowful memories were frozen forever.

Acknowledgments

The editors thank: Denmark: Copenhagen—Leif Rosenstock, The Museum for Denmark's Fight for Freedom, 1940-1945. England: London—Terry Charman, Paul Kemp, Allan Williams, Mike Willis, Imperial War Museum. France: Autun—Claudine Demeusois-Laisis, Service Culturel de la Ville d'Autun. Brion—Michel Villard. Lievin—Jean-Bernard Lavit, Service Culturel; Mairie de Lievin. Montreuil—André Rossel-Kirschen. Palisse—Albert Quzoulias.

Paris—Michel and Eliette Cabaud; Maître Serge Klarsfeld, Président de l'Association "Les fils et filles des Déportés Juifs de France"; Jean-Pierre Vittori, "Le Patriote Résistant." Rennes—Jacqueline Sainclivier. Vannes—René Diberder, Bertrand Frelaut. Germany: Berlin—Heidi Klein, Bildarchiv Preussischer Kulturbesitz; Wolfgang Streubel, Ullstein Bilderdienst. Hamburg—Jochen von Lang. Koblenz—Meinrad Nilges, Bundesarchiv. Munich—Elisabeth Heidt,

Süddeutscher Verlag Bilderdienst; Robert Hoffmann, Presseillustrationen Heinrich R. Hoffmann. Osnabrück—Karl-Walter Becker, Munin Verlag. United States: District of Columbia—Elizabeth Hill, Jim Trimble, National Archives; Eveline Nave, Library of Congress; George Snowden, Snowden Associates. New Jersey—Al Collett. Vermont—Freya von Moltke. Virginia—Ray O. Embree, Jr.; George A. Petersen, National Capital Historical Sales.

Picture Credits

Bibliography

Books

"All Gaul Is Divided . . .": Letters from Occupied France. London: Victor Gollancz, 1941.

Aron, Robert, with Georgette Elgey, *The Vichy Regime: 1940-44*. Transl. by Humphrey Hare. Boston: Beacon Press, 1969.

Barfod, Jørgen H.:
The Holocaust Failed in Denmark. Gylling, Denmark: Narayana Press, 1985.
The Museum of Denmark's Fight for Freedom 1940-1945: A Short Guide. Copenhagen: The National Museum, 1985.

Calvocoressi, Peter, Guy Wint, and John Pritchard, *Total War: The Causes and Courses of the Second World War* (rev. 2d ed.). New York: Pantheon Books, 1989.

Cobb, Richard, *French and Germans, Germans and French*. Hanover, N.H.: University Press of New England, 1983.

Dank, Milton, *The French against the French: Collaboration and Resistance*. Philadelphia: J. B. Lippincott, 1974.

Dawidowicz, Lucy S., *The War against the Jews: 1933-1945*. New York: Holt, Rinehart and Winston, 1975.

Ehrlich, Blake, *Resistance: France 1940-1945*. Boston: Little, Brown, 1965.

Elting, John R., and the Editors of Time-Life Books, *Battles for Scandinavia* (World War II series). Alexandria, Va.: Time-Life Books, 1981.

Frank, Anne, *The Diary of a Young Girl*. New York: Random House, 1952.

Goldberger, Leo, ed., *The Rescue of the Danish Jews: Moral Courage under Stress*. New York: New York University Press, 1987.

Goris, Jan-Albert, ed. and transl., *Belgium under Occupation*. New York: The Moretus Press, 1947.

Gudme, Sten, *Denmark: Hitler's "Model Protectorate."* Transl. by Jan Noble. London: Victor Gollancz, 1942.

Gutman, Israel, ed., *Encyclopedia of the Holocaust* (Vol. 2). New York: Macmillan, 1990.

Hæstrup, Jørgen, *Europe Ablaze: An Analysis of the History of the European Resistance Movements 1939-45*. Odense, Denmark: Odense University Press, 1978.

Hawes, Stephen, and Ralph White, eds., *Resistance in Europe: 1939-1945*. London: Penguin Books, 1975.

Hayes, Paul M., *Quisling: The Career and Political Ideas of Vidkun Quisling 1887-1945*. Bloomington: Indiana University Press, 1972.

Hilberg, Raul, *The Destruction of the European Jews* (3 vols.). New York: Holmes & Meier, 1985.

Homze, Edward L., *Foreign Labor in Nazi Germany*. Princeton, N.J.: Princeton University Press, 1967.

Keegan, John, *Waffen SS: The Asphalt Soldiers*. New York: Ballantine Books, 1970.

Klarsfeld, Serge, *The Children of Izieu: A Human Tragedy*. Transl. by Kenneth Jacobson. New York: Harry N. Abrams, 1985.

Kraglund, Ivar, and Arnfinn Moland, *Hjemmefront* (Vol. 6 of *Norgeikrig*). Oslo: Aschehoug, 1987.

Lemkin, Raphaël, *Axis Rule in Occupied Europe*. Washington, D.C.: Carnegie Endowment for International Peace, 1944.

Leske, Gottfried, *I Was a Nazi Flier*. Ed. by Curt Riess. New York: The Dial Press, 1941.

Lie, Arne Brun, with Robby Robinson, *Night and Fog*. New York: W. W. Norton, 1990.

Littlejohn, David:
Norway, Denmark and France (Vol. 1 of *Foreign Legions of the Third Reich*). San Jose, Calif.: R. James Bender Publishing, 1987.
Belgium, Great Britain, Holland, Italy and Spain (Vol. 2 of *Foreign Legions of the Third Reich*). San Jose, Calif.: R. James Bender Publishing, 1981.
The Patriotic Traitors: A History of Collaboration in German-Occupied Europe, 1940-45. London: William Heinemann, 1972.

Littlejohn, David, and C. M. Dodkins:
Orders, Decorations, Medals and Badges of the Third Reich. Mountain View, Calif.: R. James Bender Publishing, 1970.
Orders, Decorations, Medals and Badges of the Third Reich (Vol. 2). Mountain View, Calif.: R. James Bender Publishing, 1973.

Lottman, Herbert R., *Pétain: Hero or Traitor*. New York: William Morrow, 1985.

Moltke, Helmuth James von, *Letters to Freya: 1939-1945*. Ed. and transl. by Beate Ruhm von Oppen. New York: Alfred A. Knopf, 1990.

National Geographic, *Atlas of the World* (rev. 3d ed.). Washington, D.C.: National Geographic Society, 1970.

Nøkleby, Berit, *Holdningskamp* (Vol. 4 of *Norgeikrig*). Oslo: Aschehoug, 1986.

Paxton, Robert O., *Vichy France: Old Guard and New Order, 1940-1944*. New York: Alfred A. Knopf, 1972.

Perrault, Gilles, and Pierre Azema, *Paris under the Occupation*. Transl. by Allison Carter and Maximilian Vos. New York: The Vendome Press, 1989.

Petrow, Richard, *The Bitter Years: The Invasion and Occupation of Denmark and Norway*. New York: William Morrow, 1974.

Polnay, Peter de, *The Germans Came to Paris*. New York: Duell, Sloan and Pearce, 1943.

Pryce-Jones, David, *Paris in the Third Reich: A History of the German Occupation, 1940-1944*. New York: Holt, Rinehart and Winston, 1981.

Reitlinger, Gerald, *The SS: Alibi of a Nation*. London: Arms and Armour Press, 1981.

Rich, Norman, *Hitler's War Aims: The Establishment of the New Order* (Vol. 2). New York: W. W. Norton, 1974.

Rings, Werner, *Life with the Enemy: Collaboration and Resistance in Hitler's Europe 1939-1945*. Transl. by J. Maxwell Brownjohn. Garden City, N.Y.: Doubleday, 1982.

Seth, Ronald, *The Undaunted: The Story of Resistance in Western Europe*. London: Frederick Muller, 1956.

Shiber, Etta, with Anne Dupre and Paul Dupre, *Paris-Underground*. New York: Charles Scribner's Sons, 1943.

Snyder, Louis L., *Encyclopedia of the Third Reich*. New York: Paragon House, 1989.

Stein, George H., *The Waffen SS*. Ithaca, N.Y.: Cornell University Press, 1966.

Strassner, Peter, *European Volunteers*. Transl. by David Johnston. Winnipeg, Manitoba: J. J. Fedorowicz Publishing, 1988.

Warmbrunn, Werner, *The Dutch under German Occupation: 1940-1945*. London: Stanford University Press, 1963.

Warner, Geoffrey, *Pierre Laval and the Eclipse of France*. New York: Macmillan, 1969.

Werstein, Irving, *That Denmark Might Live: The Saga of the Danish Resistance in World War II*. Philadelphia: Macrae Smith, 1967.

Winterhager, Wilhelm Ernst, ed., *Der Kreisauer Kreis: Porträt einer Widerstandsgruppe*. Mainz: v.Hase & Koehler Verlag, 1985.

Wright, Gordon, *The Ordeal of Total War: 1939-1945*. New York: Harper & Row, 1968.

Zee, Henri A. van der, *The Hunger Winter: Occupied Holland 1944-5*. London: Jill Norman & Hobhouse, 1982.

Other Publications

Margry, Karel, "The Ambushing of SS-General Hanns Rauter." *After the Battle*, 1987, no. 56.

The Nazi Concentration Camps. Proceedings of the Fourth Yad Vashem International Historical Conference, Jerusalem, 1980. Jerusalem: Daf-Chen Press, 1984.

Index

Numerals in italics indicate an illustration of the subject mentioned.